Logistics and Manufacturing Outsourcing:

Harness Your Core Competencies

James A. Tompkins, Ph.D., Steven W. Simonson,
Bruce W. Tompkins, Brian E. Upchurch

Tompkins Press
Copyright © 2005 by Tompkins Press

TOMPKINS
PRESS

Tompkins Press
8970 Southall Road
Raleigh, NC 27616
(800) 789-1257
www.tompkinsinc.com

Logistics and Manufacturing Outsourcing: Harness Your Core
Competencies / James A. Tompkins ... [et al.].
p. cm.
Includes bibliographical references and index.
LCCN 2005901470
ISBN 1-930426-05-4

1. Business logistics — Contracting out.
2. Production management.   I. Tompkins, James A.

HD38.5.L6135 2005   658.5
QBI05-200071

DEDICATION

We would like to recognize the many people who are, and always will be, so special to us and who support us in all we do.

Thank you,
Jim, Steve, Bruce and Brian

March 31, 2005

Table of Contents

Preface

This is unlike any other outsourcing book you have seen — it is specifically crafted for logistics and manufacturing executives. When you have finished reading it, you will understand how to gain a core competency in outsourcing and what tools are needed for a successful initiative.

When we began writing this book, we knew two main truths: 1) Most organizations do not have outsourcing as a *core competency,* and this is why so many outsourcing relationships fail. You end up spending more time on *non-core competency* activities than on core, which is the exact opposite of your intention. The solution: Develop a core competency in outsourcing and then focus on your organization's core competencies. 2) The four authors of this book have nearly 100 years of solid experience in logistics and manufacturing outsourcing — either as providers, consultants, clients, attorneys or expert witnesses. In other words, we've seen outsourcing from all angles, and it isn't always a pretty picture. This makes us uniquely qualified to teach companies how to harness the power behind outsourcing.

Chapter 1 presents the background of logistics and manufacturing outsourcing. Chapter 2 covers the challenges being faced by executives today, and Chapter 3 provides the outsourcing opportunity to address these challenges. Chapters 4 through 12 explore the process of outsourcing that Tompkins Associates has developed over the past three decades. Next, Chapter 13 looks at some of the risks inherent in outsourcing and how to mitigate them. We conclude with Chapter 14, the future of outsourcing in logistics and manufacturing and a call to action.

You will find several features of the book to be particularly useful:

- Real-life case studies of successful and "not so successful" outsourcing;

- An "Elevator Speech" summary of the entire book in the appendix. This is the perfect remedy for the "I've got a captive audience and need to state my case in three minutes" panic; and
- A list of key risks associated with outsourcing and how to avoid them.

We have worked hard to give you the tools you need to harness your core competencies and enjoy success in logistics and manufacturing outsourcing.

All the best,
Jim, Steve, Bruce and Brian

Logistics and Manufacturing Outsourcing

INTRODUCTION

It's no secret that the world's most successful companies — like Dell, Wal-Mart, and Sony — owe much of that success to outsourcing. In their search for increased competitiveness and success in today's global marketplace, companies are either considering outsourcing as an avenue or they have already decided to pursue it. The word is everywhere. For example, a search on *Yahoo!* alone for "outsourcing" yields more than 2.6 million results.

Interestingly, if you narrow that search to "successful outsourcing," there are more than 416,000 websites that claim to have the secret to successful outsourcing. A search for "outsourcing" on amazon.com reveals more than 4,000 book titles. However, the multitude of websites and books claiming to help businesses succeed with outsourcing indicates that a company cannot simply announce, "We're going to outsource everything we can," and expect to reap the benefits. Yet that's what so many companies are doing.

Consider the experience of a well-known casual clothing producer that decided to go the outsourcing route to boost its market share and land a lucrative contract with a large retailer like Wal-Mart. It created a department with the sole responsibility of managing outsourcing relationships, and that department is now the gatekeeper for all outsourcing providers that want to do business with that company. That department is largely comprised of experts (on the functional competencies being outsourced) who understand the outsource vs. insource question, know the solicitation process, and realize the importance of maintaining ongoing relationships with outsourcing providers. They have years of experience with outsourcing contracts and dos and don'ts, and they bear various outsourcing war wounds. Yet for them, outsourcing is not producing the desired results, and many are either frustrated or questioning the value of outsourcing altogether.

What has eluded this company—and others like it—is this: Outsourcing is a management tool that shifts the organizational structure of companies. It is a business transformation process that can create great opportunity for improved performance, but it can also create great opportunity for problems, issues, and, ultimately, failure. In the search for core competencies and non-core competencies to outsource, it is easy to overlook the fact that outsourcing itself is a competency. As such, it must be approached with business process knowledge and effective outsourcing processes experience to reap its full benefits.

What does this mean for the clothing producer? Well, unless someone within the company who has been overlooked suddenly shows up at the conference room door with a résumé full of outsourcing process expertise, their best bet is to consider looking outside the walls of their own company. There are companies that possess a wealth of outsourcing knowledge. They've been in the trenches for decades, before the term "outsourcing" was even coined, and they know the ropes. They realize that for most companies, outsourcing is not a core competency. These outsourcing specialists know that they can offer their expertise to those who have not developed it themselves, integrating it with the knowledge and experience company insiders bring to the table.

Outsourcing outsourcing? Is that possible? Sure it is. Many companies believe that the manufacturing and logistics experts within a company are the natural choices for finding third-party manufacturing and logistics providers. In some cases, this may be true. But in most cases, these experts have been busy with manufacturing and logistics operations and are overwhelmed when it comes time to hand those processes over to someone outside the company. A company with outsourcing as a core competency can work with these experts, harnessing their knowledge and experience and using it to develop and manage logistics and manufacturing outsourcing relationships.

Why logistics and manufacturing? The answer to that question goes back to the amazon.com search. We took the list of 4,000 titles, reviewed the top books, and learned something very important: the books in the list concentrate on IT, HR, payroll, and marketing. We found, in effect, no books that focused on how to outsource manufacturing and logistics. Those that mentioned these functions treated them as either afterthoughts or also-rans. Amazing! The most profitable, well-known, and highly touted companies have gotten where they are today by outsourcing logistics and manufacturing, and no one is really telling the story. Talk about an eye-opener!

In our desire to fill that void, we share our lessons learned here to help companies that want to successfully outsource either logistics or manufacturing (or both) but don't know how to go about getting it done. This chapter examines the history of outsourcing, emerging trends, what we see happening, and what we envision for the future.

Logistics Outsourcing Today

In a recent survey of international business executives in manufacturing and retail, AMR found that 34% were not using or even considering a Logistics Service Provider (LSP), citing loss of control, lack of sector knowledge and potential damage to customer satisfaction. Even among the 58% of companies currently using an LSP, the ability to let go of a function that traditionally has been handled internally is poor. Among those companies that do outsource, only 4% outsource all of their logistics; 57% outsource less than half of their activities.

Why? "Logistics is the last contact point with the customer in the supply chain," AMR observes. "As an active participant in the transfer of control to a third party, users need to feel confident that their customers' changing requirements will be met to maintain and enhance customer relationships and the company brand image." In other words, companies that outsource logistics don't want someone who just drops goods at the loading docks and runs. Instead, they want a provider who treats the outsourcer's customer as their own and takes just as much care in ensuring their satisfaction.

AMR found that those who do outsource are having far better results than might be expected, given all the hand wringing. About a third report that customer satisfaction levels actually improved; only 7% report a decline. About a quarter (24%) report that personnel costs declined, and 17% report that other operating costs declined. Another 10% cite improvements in inventory management.

"The most successful businesses balance customer demands with financial necessities by setting performance goals and executing against them," AMR Analyst Gerald McNerney writes. "Although they recognize that logistics execution is vital to their business, many companies lack the ability to have the people, processes and technologies in place internally to efficiently scale and manage all logistics execution." McNerney concludes that, increasingly, companies will have no choice but to outsource their logistics activities.[1]

EVOLUTION OF LOGISTICS AND MANUFACTURING OUTSOURCING

While outsourcing is a relatively new term (coined some time in the late 1980s), the practice of outsourcing logistics and manufacturing dates back hundreds of years.

In pre-Renaissance Italy, merchants in the province of Lombardy used paper documentation, known as Lombards, as receipts for inventory stored in common (third-party) warehouses. After making a purchase, customers would take a Lombard to a centrally located warehouse to retrieve the merchandise. With this system, merchants avoided paying the prices for shipping products to the market or directly to customers and customers used these precursors to paper money to collect their purchases quickly. In Latin America, this system is still in use today.

For centuries, the ships that sailed the world's oceans were common carriers. They transported and stored goods so that a manufacturer could focus on producing goods. Logistics outsourcing grew as transportation networks developed and product markets expanded. The Interstate Commerce Act of 1887 ensured that railroad monopolies practiced fair pricing. This gave small businesses the same access to (and the same price for) third-party transportation as large corporations. The use of freight cars and railroad depots as warehouse storage points and the use of co-op grain elevators to store harvests are prime examples of outsourced warehousing activities.

Then came World War II. The households it disrupted created a demand for storing household goods. The multi-story buildings erected or modified for such use were quickly converted after the war to general purpose warehousing, marking the birth of short-term contracts for public warehousing as we know them today. These public warehouse operations provided manufacturers the means to reevaluate their practice of maintaining their own proprietary warehouse operations in each marketplace.

Manufacturing has also been outsourced for a number of centuries. Do you think Dell's use of contract manufacturers to produce their made-to-order computers is new? Think again. For centuries, tradesmen and artisans took customers' orders before they did the work and then hired extra craftsmen to make what had been ordered. Before and during the Industrial revolution, contracting dominated the economic organization of production. Historical documents indicate that in 19th century England, specialized metal manufacturing functions were often contracted.[2]

Then, from the mid-19th century until about 20 years ago, contracting was put aside as mega-corporations were created with vertical integration, or the full internalization of operations for growth. Ford Motor Company is a good example. When Henry Ford realized how much glass was needed to build his automobiles, he decided to acquire a glass factory.

The key measure of success at that time was revenue. The belief was that doing everything within the corporation generated more sales.

Things began to change again in the 1980s and 1990s for both logistics and manufacturing. The need for service-providing specialists was on the rise, and businesses were competing to provide logistics services. Federal Express, under CEO Fred Smith, revolutionized the way people thought about logistics outsourcing and the way we have conducted business ever since. Federal Express quickly became a success because of their overnight delivery. It became possible and then necessary to deliver almost anything, anywhere overnight.

During that period, the manufacturing sector began to realize that their organizations had become too large and complex to be responsive or effective. Company leaders were unable to effectively manage the scope and breadth of operations and achieve the necessary levels of performance. Thus, size and complexity became a detriment to profitability. In their search for solutions, they hit upon the age-old practice of contracting. Before long, companies like Flextronics and Solectron were providing electronics manufacturers with the actual manufactured goods to be branded under more familiar names.

Looming on the horizon during this time was the Internet. It has compelled not only retailers and manufacturers to overhaul their practices, but logistics providers as well. Consumers want their products cheaper and quicker, and this demand shapes the way we do business today. This has created the acceleration of outsourcing as an accepted management tool, fueled by the need for intense focus on profitability and not just cost cutting, and by the growth in size and capabilities of contract providers. True economies of scale are possible with many of today's service and product providers.

TRENDS IN THE PAST TEN YEARS

For the past decade, organizations have been downsizing, right-sizing, and reengineering in efforts to improve efficiency and financial performance. These techniques have generally reduced costs and assets. However, they have not truly addressed the work that needs to be done, who is going to do it, and if it is really a core competency or not.

Outsourcing, when done properly, reduces the work required of the organization and improves the efficiency and effectiveness of processes. Because some of the biggest names in business have done it right, outsourcing is being viewed as a means to higher profitability and larger market share. As such, the percentage of companies that view outsourced manufacturing and logistics services as viable alternatives to internal operations has increased over the last 10 years. As a result, we have noticed a number of trends, including:

- Increased spending for outside warehousing and outbound transportation;
- Improvement in outsource provider capabilities;
- Greater use of software and technology solutions;
- Increased competition amongst contractors;
- More short-term outsourcing projects;
- New outsourcing products and innovations for the marketplace; and
- A shift in overall management thinking about ownership and assets.

These trends are discussed in the sections that follow.

Increased Spending

At one time, companies sought to outsource functions like IT, HR, and mailroom services and budgeted accordingly. In the past few years, however, the percentage of company budgets spent on outside warehousing and outbound transportation is on the rise. One of the reasons for this trend is the ever-increasing pace of global trade and the popularity of offshore contract electronics manufacturing. Companies are contracting with logistics consultants to untangle global supply chains, integrate and monitor international shipping, and help companies weave their way through increasingly complicated product supply channels.[3]

Another reason for these expenditures is that companies are learning that these operations are not necessarily core functions. Core functions are an organization's core competency, the unique business functions that allow the organization to be successful. They are the critical activities included in an organization's vision statement that allow it to thrive. For a research organization, the core function is research. For a manufacturing organization, the core function is manufacturing. And for a distribution organization, the core function is distribution. Now, the research organization may also do some manufacturing and distribution, but its core function is research. In fact, the research organization may do manufacturing, distribution, finance, marketing, procurement, information technology, human resources and more, but research remains its core.

> ## Outsourcing is Like a Box of Chocolates
>
> Jean-Marc Gorce makes chocolate truffles by hand at XOX Truffles in San Francisco. This small shop has been rated as one of the top ten in the United States. In addition to being a chef, Jean-Marc is also an entrepreneur and an innovator.
>
> Jean-Marc recently started selling his chocolates in attractive gold and blue boxes. His wife came up with the design, and he found a company in the Philippines that could produce the boxes in the small volume they needed for a good price.
>
> Jean-Marc's gold and blue boxes are an example of successful outsourcing. Jean-Marc sells chocolates, not boxes. The design and production of chocolates is his core competency. He has outsourced box production to improve his operational efficiency without sacrificing his reputation as a maker of superlative chocolates.[4]

Improved Capabilities, Software Solutions, and Increased Competition

Outsourcing providers are becoming more capable, using technology and software, including the Internet and specialized applications, to create innovative solutions. At the same time, companies want to work with fewer contractors to streamline communications and reduce interactions. There is heightened competition amongst contractors due to this rationing of service providers, which has outsource providers offering an increasingly integrated set of services that cover a broader range of functions.

Take Flextronics International, for example. In September 2003, the Singapore-based company was first on the list of the top 100 contract manufacturers published by *Electronic Business*.[5] When Flextronics went public in 1994, it basically manufactured electronics components. Now the company's services range from design engineering through manufacturing and assembly to distribution and warehousing, and they also offer the installation and maintenance of communications networks.

It is important to note here that because so many companies have outsourced manufacturing to Flextronics, which is located in Singapore, many executives, pundits, and politicians tend to equate outsourcing with offshoring. This is a common mistake. Yes, many outsource providers are located overseas — in Asia or India, for example. However, outsourcing is not offshoring. Offshoring is an outsourcing option, just as contracting to a domestic service provider is an outsourcing option. Companies need to look at the total supply chain costs and make their service provider decisions based on what will best achieve long-term goals. For example, earlier in this chapter, we mentioned that logistics outsourcing was growing in popularity because of global trade and offshoring. So far, it has been demonstrated in various instances that using U.S.-based logistics providers has had the optimum impact on bottom lines.[6]

More Short-Term Projects

Another trend that has emerged in the last decade is that companies are increasingly using service providers for short-term projects rather than creating long-term relationships. This can be a good thing if a company needs a quick fix. For example, a software company releasing a new version of its premier program that wants to offer free telephone support for a limited time is a prime candidate for successful short-term outsourcing (by using a third-party call center). The same may be said for a company that is selling a limited run of a product and decides to outsource its packaging. However, an appliance manufacturer that wants to outsource the production of one of its smaller volume products may be better off fostering a long-term relationship with the outsourcer so that the customer does not perceive the product as unreliable. Economics today can favor short-term outsourcing decisions, so management time, resources and capital are not expended in short-term or high-risk operations.

New Products and Innovation

Digital radio, chips for mobile communications, a silicone adhesive — these are among the numerous products that have been introduced in the last few years. Nothing stops innovation. However, as much as companies want to exploit creativity and technology, they also are looking for ways to curb upfront capital investment.

Their search creates opportunities to use outsourced manufacturing and logistics to do more with less. For example, computer giant Hewlett-Packard, in an attempt to capitalize on the popularity of digital music in 2003, tried to develop a digital music player. However, late that year, the company decided that it could get into the digital music market faster if it outsourced the player but branded it in-house. The result was a deal announced in January 2004 for HP to utilize Apple to produce iPods under the HP brand name.

Shift in Management Thinking

In the last few years, company leaders have changed their views about ownership and control of assets. They are realizing that relinquishing the tight reins they have held on costly assets will increase growth and improve earnings. At the same time, they continue to seek:

- Workforce reduction;
- Freedom from a restrictive labor environment;
- Expanded geographic coverage;
- Operational flexibility;
- Reduced cycle time/improved responsiveness; and
- Logistics operations cost reduction.

However, they are shifting their thinking away from simply downsizing or expanding into new areas without careful thought and planning to acquire what they seek. They have recognized that there is a second step that must follow selling off assets and shedding workers. Many of them believe that outsourcing is that step.

WHAT DOES ALL THIS MEAN?

From these trends, several conclusions can be drawn. First, the decision on whether to outsource or not has almost been made for many company leaders. They have no choice but to outsource. Yet, for outsourcing to work for these companies, they either must become very good at outsourcing or they must be willing to outsource the outsourcing process to experts. This is because the winner in this game is the company that is best at outsourcing. Second, competition has made outsourcing a viable option for many more companies and for many more logistics and manufacturing functions. Outsourcing is paying off in areas we didn't even dream about 10 years ago. Lastly, pressures for improved financial results have never been greater. This pressure has created a surge of interest in outsourcing functions where bottom line improvement potential exists. These trends and conclusions have shaped our vision of the future of outsourcing.

FUTURE VISION OF OUTSOURCING

The future is difficult to predict for a variety of reasons. For one thing, any predictions cannot be based on the past, even though the past is all most company leaders know. For another, while change is expected, the kind of change companies experience is, for the most part, the unexpected. For example, who knew, even 10 years ago, that people would be able to connect to companies all around the world through their computers and not only communicate with them, but conduct business with them as well? In 1996, the World Wide Web was mainly a new place for businesses to advertise; now, an infinite number of programs and hardware at different locations can be controlled by one application that is accessed via the Web. Again, who could have predicted that?

That is not to say that no one should try to predict the future. It just means that when a company starts making plans, it must take into account the unforeseen. With that in mind, we venture to make a few statements about our vision of the future.

First, the percentage of budgets spent on outsourcing and contracting will continue to rise for many years to come. Secondly, outsourcing providers will be the leaders in IT and technology innovation as companies reduce their investments in technology and extend their capabilities through outsourcing arrangements. Moreover, outsourcers will bring a new dimension to the marketplace in terms of speed to market and rapid deliveries to support the conduct of business over the web. There will be a growing sensitivity to product life cycle as outsourcing is used earlier in the cycle to minimize upfront capital investment and later in the cycle when the investment is no longer justified. The reach of outsourcing will extend beyond manufacturing or logistics to encompass the entire supply chain, and industry-specific solutions providers will continue to grow. Service providers will become the leading supply chain strategists.

Companies will use outsourcers to gain access to the global talent pool. With that will come greater contact between service providers and companies' customers. These developments will contribute to the maturing of the outsourcing movement and increase the emphasis on building relationships.

So, the future of logistics and manufacturing outsourcing overall is bright. However, to bask in this glow, companies need to pursue it with careful planning and complete understanding of their business processes and core competencies. When applied properly, outsourcing can help companies meet today's business challenges head on and with measurable success. To understand how to make that happen, we need to look at today's business challenges. This will be the topic of the next chapter.

---

1 Bernadette Heame. "AMR: Outsourcing Logistics Works Better than You Think," *eye for chem.* February 27, 2003. http://www.eyeforchem.com/index.asp?src=hn &nli=og-c&nld=2/27/2003&news=35346

2 Simon Domberger. *The Contracting Organization* (New York: 1998), p. 8.

3 Robert Guy Matthews. "Globalization is Creating U.S. Logistics Jobs." *The Wall Street Journal,* 1 Mar. 2004.

4 Michael Bean. "The Pitfalls of Outsourcing Programming: Why Some Software Companies Confuse the Box with the Chocolates." *Forio Business Simulations,* 2001-2004. http://www.forio.com/outsourcing.htm

5 Bill Roberts. "Top 100 Contract Manufacturers." *Electronic Business.* September 1, 2003. http://www.reed-electronics.com/eb-mag/index.asp?layout=article&article-id=CA319074&industryid=2116&rid=0&rme=0&cfd=1

6 Matthews, "Globalization."

Have you ever been on an elevator with an important business colleague and wished you could quickly and eloquently communicate your thoughts? This "On the Elevator" summary at the end of each chapter will help you make the best use of the three-minute elevator ride. An appendix to this book combines these summaries.

ON THE ELEVATOR

Outsourcing is a management tool that shifts the organizational structure of companies. It is a business transformation process that can create great opportunity for improved performance, but it can also create great opportunity for problems, issues, and, ultimately, failure. While outsourcing is a relatively new term, the idea has been around for a long time. It was a part of doing business in Renaissance Italy and 19th century England.

After World War II, it fell out of favor as companies transformed themselves into vertical enterprises, trying to be all things to all people. But in the last few decades and particularly in the last 10 years, trends such as downsizing, right-sizing, consolidating, and reengineering combined with the explosion of the Internet have shifted the focus of company leaders back to outsourcing. Software and technology offerings have expanded, new products and innovations have grown, and management's thinking has shifted to an understanding that some assets are costly and can hurt earnings.

As a result, more and more companies are eyeing outsourcing as a viable method for improving speed to market and increasing market share. The percentage of budgets spent on outsourcing is rising, providers are becoming more capable, contractors are experiencing heightened competition, and the percentage of companies outsourcing manufacturing and logistics services is on a sharp increase. This is a new development, except in the small electronics manufacturing sector. Until now, the focus of outsourcing has been HR, IT, and marketing. This is obvious if you do any kind of search on the Web for outsourcing. It is also the reason we have decided to write this book. Look at it this way: many of the most profitable, well-known, and highly touted companies have gotten where they are by outsourcing logistics and manufacturing.

So, with all the stories of outsourcing success and the excitement they generate, it's no wonder that so many companies are either already outsourcing or plan to outsource in the next year. However, in the search for core competencies and non-core competencies to outsource, it easy to overlook the fact that outsourcing itself is a competency. As such, it must be approached with business process knowledge and effective outsourcing process experience to reap its full benefits. It also requires a thorough understanding of today's business challenges and how outsourcing can be used effectively to manage them.

2 Today's Business Challenges

INTRODUCTION

A recent book, *No Boundaries: Break Through to Supply Chain Excellence*, begins with this simple statement: "This is not your parents' economy."[1] This is so true. The age of mass production and vertical enterprises our parents knew is gone, and business is not as much fun as it used to be.

Competition, globalization, technology, pace, and the capital markets have all had a major impact on business today. Everyone in business organizations has too much to do and not enough time to do it. CEOs are pressed, but so too are those who hold entry-level positions. Downsizing has resulted in having fewer people in the organization, but the reality is, in today's complex business environment, we have much more work to accomplish in our quest to achieve customer satisfaction, business growth, and increased profitability.

Our quest is not that different from that of our predecessors; however, the means of succeeding in it have changed radically. Today, companies must make critical decisions about what they really want to do themselves and what they want others to do for them. Otherwise, they will fall by the wayside, beaten by their broken supply chains.

To deliver maximum customer value, customization, and satisfaction — all while reducing inventory, trimming lead times, and reducing costs — companies must be able to identify their core competencies and trim away the excess fat of processes impacting company performance and profitability. At the same time, companies must meet today's business challenges quickly and efficiently.

What are today's business challenges? Simply put, they are:

- Shifting channel structures and business relationships;
- Customer satisfaction;

- Speeding time to market;
- Information technology;
- Globalization;
- Virtual factories; and
- Outsourcing.

This chapter tackles these challenges with an emphasis on *why* they are challenges and the basic requirements for meeting them.

SHIFTING CHANNEL STRUCTURES AND BUSINESS RELATIONSHIPS

In the last decade, organizations have de-layered, reengineered, downsized, and deverticalized. For some, the primary objective of their restructuring initiatives was to reduce overhead to create cost savings for greater competitiveness. Others saw the flattening of organizations as a way to gain freedom from bureaucracy, to speed up communications, and to develop a customer-focused culture.

Today's company has morphed into a diversified entity that competes, collaborates, and co-creates in a network of other companies. These entities strive to become virtual organizations. They are forging new relationships, enhancing their supply chains, increasing organizational responsiveness, and focusing on bottom line results.

All these developments have a mind-boggling impact on channel structures and relationships. They call for business process reorganization, and they require new kinds of partnerships that leap over one of the highest hurdles in the business world — the "us vs. them" mentality. Ultimately, those who truly understand how to nurture and continuously evolve partnership-like relationships with their external suppliers and service providers will triumph. This is the challenge of business relationships and shifting channel structures.

CUSTOMER SATISFACTION

Customization, customer choice, customer value, customer relationship management and customer-centric thinking are increasingly being used to describe business focus. This is a radical change from the enterprisewide focus of the last decade. Now, customer satisfaction is paramount. It requires companies to divest themselves of self-interest and concentrate on the needs, expectations, and perceptions of those who buy and use their products. What happens when customers' thoughts, wants, and needs drive innovation and flow of goods and services from raw materials suppliers to retailers and ultimately back to those customers? You have customer satisfaction.

The specific steps for achieving and increasing customer satisfaction are:

- Reducing costs;
- Increasing quality;
- Promoting teamwork; and
- Responding to customer needs.

Simplifying the processes of manufacturing and distribution, reducing waste and inventory, and increasing efficiency all reduce costs. To increase quality, a clear, measurable definition of the level of quality and reliability that the customer expects for the price paid must be communicated to all involved in getting a product to the customer. This establishes standards and implements process control at all levels, along with keeping everyone involved focused on the customers and their needs.

None of this can be done without teamwork—the collaboration between internal and external functions. Teamwork removes boundaries between supply chain links, creates new practices that anticipate individual customer needs and expectations, and provides customers with products and services they perceive as unique and valuable. These requirements are not to be taken lightly; they require a great deal of effort and intense cooperation.

Partnership Creates Higher Customer Satisfaction

United Service Source, Inc. (USSI), an international company specializing in the installation and maintenance for a wide range of services in the commercial and government sectors, has realized a significant increase in customer retention, satisfaction, and expansion since partnering with Choice Logistics to take advantage of its global network of logistics services.

USSI once managed its logistics operations internally, and as a result, non-revenue generating activity consumed valuable resources. Since partnering with Choice, USSI has improved its Service Level Agreements (SLAs) by 100%, increased its overall customer satisfaction rating by 50%, and realized a 50% decrease in annual financial exposure. Choice's distribution model has created quicker turnaround times, consistently exceeding customer expectations and delivering a rapid ROI for both USSI and its clients.[2]

SPEEDING TIME TO MARKET

Today's business environment demands speed and more speed. This phenomenon is pervasive. Fewer and fewer of us drive below or at the speed limit. Starting up our servers and logging into e-mail seems to take forever, but in reality, it takes about eight seconds. We grind our teeth when we're put on hold and told that our wait time will be one minute.

The Internet and the Web have helped create this sense of urgency. They turned the notion of immediate orders into reality, and now we all want our products to arrive almost as quickly. A frequent comment from clients is "People click and they expect the order's shipping time to be just as quick."

The key to increasing speed to market is the creation of supply chains that focus on reducing customer lead-time, production lead-time, and manufacturing lead-time. These supply chains are complex — created through partnerships with suppliers, outsource providers, and third parties. They must be flexible, meeting all customer satisfaction requirements through robust design methods enabled by real-time decision tools, as well as manufacturing and distribution synthesis.

The supply chains must be built carefully, with the correct balance of insourcing and outsourcing. If these supply chains are assembled through hasty decisions, they will not work. That's what makes increasing speed to market such a challenge.

INFORMATION TECHNOLOGY

Many of us now have a difficult time remembering the days before voice mail and e-mail. LANs, WANs, VPNs, intranets, extranets, video conferencing, whiteboarding, streaming, and webcasts — these once mysterious terms have become a part of our everyday business lives. IT can sometimes make us crazy, especially when it doesn't move as quickly as we want it to, which is ironic, since it is what has prompted us to demand speed in everything we do. IT is the driving force that has brought our world closer. Applied correctly, IT brings out the best in our people and harnesses creativity in team and individual environments.

IT moves forward faster every day. The Web and the Internet are now places for dialogues and relationships, places to resolve differences between systems and platforms, and tools for learning more about individual customers. Enterprise application integrators (EAIs) and web application servers are tying disparate systems and programs together. Auto ID, wireless communications technology and business software have been standardized; system integrators have written custom interfaces to allow the exchange of data between programs. All of these advances level the playing field for competitors, make it more difficult to establish a brand, and increase the importance of providing quality service.

With IT, companies can extend their market reach and accomplish things beyond the scope of imagination. However, they can also make costly mistakes if they do not use these "new powers" wisely. It's important to remember that IT will not solve a company's ills by itself, but instead it is a critical tool to be applied judiciously so that it facilitates communication between different groups and companies.

GLOBALIZATION

New trade agreements, individual countries partnering with each other to produce and export goods, international e-commerce, and web applications have created a 24/7, on-demand, global marketplace. Politics and technology took us down this path, but the current focus on reducing costs and increasing profits has cemented it into a requirement for doing business today. On February 26, 2004, Jeffrey R. Immelt, Chairman of GE, had this to say to a group of investors about globalization: "Globalization has a bad name. But the world is inextricably global. We win by exporting and we win by sourcing."[3]

Immelt is right. There's no going back now. If customers can get products quicker and cheaper because they're being manufactured while they sleep by workers in China that accept lower pay, then those are the products they are going to buy. If companies can widen the gap between expenditures and revenues and turn a greater profit by using Indian engineers to design their products, then that's what they're going to do. Globalization is like technology. It can reap huge benefits for companies that use it properly and wisely.

At the same time, many seem to confuse the topics of globalization and outsourcing. Globalization is reality. If the best strategy is to combine globalization and outsourcing, fine, but it must be clear that these are two different topics.

What we're seeing today, though, are companies that equate globalization with moving as many functions offshore as possible. Offshore manufacturing and assembly are working for many companies, such as

The Flip Side of Globalization

For 16 years, a giant, multinational corporation has quietly moved more research overseas, hiring hundreds of young foreign engineers for work previously done in the company's home country. This spring, this company will open a new styling and design studio in a foreign country. Is this Ford or GM? Dell? IBM? Not hardly. This is Toyota and it has almost completed the Toyota Technical Center (TTC) USA in Ann Arbor, Michigan.

Graduates from Purdue, Lawrence Tech, University of Michigan, and other U.S. engineering schools work in the 100-acre campus. These engineers work with Toyota suppliers and a Toyota chief engineer, creating future models of the Avalon and Solara passenger cars and the Sienna minivan.

Think of this as the flip side of globalization. Today's political rhetoric focuses on the export of U.S. jobs to places like India, China and Mexico, and it ignores the fact that Japanese and European companies have transformed the automotive landscape in Michigan in the last 20 years.

Toyota Technical Center now has 634 employees, 506 of them in Michigan. TTC's workforce includes 99 Japanese expatriates, which means the ratio has changed from 80% Japanese 10 years ago to more than 80% American now, says Tadashi Yamashina, TTC president. A new styling center in Ann Arbor—a satellite to Toyota's main U.S. design shop is in Newport Beach, California—will be completed this spring, adding a few more people.[4]

automakers and textile producers. However, in some cases, it may not be as cost effective as it appears on paper to send jobs overseas. For example, there are beginning to be questions about how well it works to send technical support and customer service overseas. Dell has moved customer care back to the U.S. after discovering that the technical staff in India did not have the experience necessary to handle many of the calls.[5] Other companies did not realize that it would be difficult for someone who might not own a washing machine to provide information to a customer half a world away who does own one.

To answer the challenge of globalization, companies must know when to take advantage of what it has to offer and to think carefully about its impacts on customer satisfaction. Cultural differences, English idiomatic expressions, and differences in engineering studies here and abroad can eat into the promise of cost savings. Exploiting the benefits of globalization requires holism, not just a quick glance at a spreadsheet.

VIRTUAL FACTORIES

Virtual factories are the product of focused factories, deverticalization, ease of sharing information all over the world, the Web, outsourcing, globalization, and the demand for increasing speed to market. These entities gather, organize, select, synthesize, and distribute information and parts with information technology, such as electronic data interchange (EDI), the Internet, or a combination of technology. Production and scheduling, along with shipping and supply ordering, are conducted in real-time or via the Web.

In virtual factories, the rules of economies of scale and scope of ability do not apply. Instead, the foundation for their processes are relationships with customers and strategic partners, with an eye to anticipating and handling inventory, production costs, product design, capacity planning, training, and other aspects of manufacturing. The transformation of huge, outdated manufacturing monoliths into these sleek, lean, flexible, and agile operations presents a major challenge.

OUTSOURCING

Outsourcing is today's most unique business challenge. This is because outsourcing is both a solution to other business challenges and a challenge in its own right. Numerous companies have had considerable success with outsourcing secondary non-core functions (audit, landscaping, payroll, food services, janitorial, etc.), and so a logical extension is to

Wharton and Boston Consulting Group: Outsourcing is Here to Stay

Experts at Wharton and the Boston Consulting Group say outsourcing is no longer a tactical option that can help a firm save a few dollars here and there. Rather, it has emerged as a strategic necessity in an era when opportunities offered by "low-cost countries," such as China, India, or Mexico, abound. Indeed, these experts have concluded that outsourcing will continue to move forward and transform national economies in both the developed and developing worlds in the process.

"It's the classic 'makes vs. buys' question," says Morris Cohen, professor of manufacturing and logistics at Wharton. "Do I make something internally or buy it in the marketplace, and how do I add value most effectively? This is a problem that's been studied in economics and management for decades. This is not a new issue, and it's not one that will ever go away."

What has changed, Cohen says, is that more companies are engaged in more outsourcing than before — and they are doing it in novel ways. "The idea of moving things offshore and outside the boundary of the firm — more of that has been happening around processes you would never have thought possible. Having somebody in India answer calls — who would have ever thought of that?"

Hal Sirkin, senior vice president and director in Boston Consulting Group's Chicago office and head of the firm's global operations practice, emphasizes that "leveraging low-cost countries" is not only about reducing costs. "It cuts across a number of dimensions. It doesn't mean your total cost will be cheaper if you can find someone who can make something cheaper. Having a long supply chain is not as cheap [as a short one]. You can't look at leveraging low-cost countries as just finding the purest, lowest cost widget. It affects so much of your business and your customers."[6]

pursue primary non-core functions (logistics, information technology, marketing, manufacturing, etc.).

For example, the last decade saw a significant growth of 3PLs and manufacturing outsourcing, and this trend continues. A 2003 survey conducted by Accenture and Northeastern University found that the percentage of large manufacturers using 3PL services increased to 83% from 65% in 2002.[7] Contract manufacturing, once seen as something that was only used by electronics manufacturers, has expanded to include beer and automobile production.[8] IT outsourcing continues to grow in leaps and bounds, despite outcries from industry commentators that it either doesn't work or it hurts profits.[9] According to the Yankee Group, applications targeting business activities outside the enterprise are expected to account for an average of 34% of tech spending in 2004.[10]

Unfortunately, outsourcing primary non-core functions has resulted in major failures. In fact, more than one-quarter of all outsourcing deals fail in the first year.[11] For companies that have experienced these failures, outsourcing is viewed as an organizational setback. They wring their hands and moan that outsourcing is something that just doesn't work. In reality, however, outsourcing does work — when a company knows what it is doing. Instead, the problem is that these organizations lack a core competency in the process of outsourcing. Many didn't do their homework before jumping on the outsourcing bandwagon. They pursued outsourcing of primary non-core functions as if they were secondary non-core functions.

Organizations that provide secondary non-core functions offer straightforward, end-to-end packaged services that require very little customization. It's a very basic process: someone in the organization walks the property with the landscape service provider, and they send the company a two-page proposal, a monthly fee, and a one-page contract. The company signs the contract, the provider does the landscaping and invoicing per that contract, and the company pays the provider. Very simple, and the landscaping looks great. So, then the company decides to outsource primary non-core functions, they use the same simple approach for this strategic outsource as they did for the secondary non-core outsource. And what happens? The company becomes a poster child for the failure of outsourcing.

To take the plunge into outsourcing primary non-core functions without a robust outsourcing process will not only prevent an organization from achieving the benefits from outsourcing, but will also result in a major setback to the organization. Believe it or not, we have seen multi-million dollar logistics outsourcing efforts where the process was little more than the approach for the landscape outsourcing described above. For outsourcing to work, a solid, up-front effort is required to identify the functions to be outsourced, so that the right processes that have the best returns are considered. Once the identification has been completed, then an organization's outsourcing process must be rigorously applied to assure that the potential benefits of outsourcing are achieved. This is the true challenge—making outsourcing a core competency so that it truly is a solution for other business challenges. When you do this, outsourcing is no longer a challenge, but an opportunity.

1 James A. Tompkins, Ph.D., *No Boundaries: Break Through to Supply Chain Excellence*, 2003, Tompkins Press (Raleigh, NC), p. iii.

2 "USSI Customer Satisfaction at an All-Time High Since Tapping Choice Logistics; Unparalleled Service Leads To Unparalleled Results." *Businesswire*, 1 March 2004. http://home.businesswire.com/portal/site/google/index.jsp?ndmViewId= news_view&newsId=20040301005433&newsLang=en

3 "Immelt's Big Cheer for Globalization," *BusinessWeek Online*, 27 February 2004. http://www.businessweek.com/bwdaily/dnflash/feb2004/nf20040227_2342_db 039.htm

4 Tom Walsh. "Globalization Brings Work to Michigan," *Detroit Free Press*, 27 February 2004. http://globalization.about.com/gi/dynamic/offsite.htm?site= http://www.freep.com/money/business/walsh27%5F20040227.htm

5 Jesse Drucker and Ken Brown. "Some Companies Let Customers Choose Where Work is Done." *Mlive.com*, 9 March 2004. http://www.mlive.com/newsflash/ business/index.ssf?/newsflash/get_story.ssf?/cgi-free/getstory_ssf.cgi? f0051_BC_WSJ–Outsourcing-Choi&&news&newsflash-financial

6 "It's time to talk sense about outsourcing." *SearchCIO.com*, 1 March 2004. http://searchcio.techtarget.com/originalContent/0,289142,sid19_gci953020,00.html

7 "Four Out of Five Manufacturers Surveyed." *DC Velocity*. January, 2004, p. 3.

8 "Scottish & Newcastle to Shut Edinburgh Plant." *Financial Times* (London). 18 Feb. 2004; "Hyundai, Kia Refit Assembly Lines to Raise Profitability." *Korea Herald, Financial Times Information Limited – Asian Business Wire*, 25 February 2004.

9 Paul A. Straussman. "Most Outsourcing is Still for Losers." *Computer World*. 2 February 2004, p. 25.

10 "Analyst Watch: Spending Looks Outward." *Information Week*. 23 February 2004. http://www.informationweek.com/story/showArticle.jhtml;jsessionid=JTKZ5PR OXCBNYQSNDBGCKHY?articleID=18100092.

11 Patricia MacInnis. "Warped Expectations Lead to Outsourcing Failures." *Computing Canada*, 11 April 2003. http://www.findarticles.com/cf_dls/m0CGC/ 7_29/100202216/p1/article.jhtml.

ON THE ELEVATOR

Business is not as much fun as it used to be. There's too much to do and not enough time to do it. Competition, globalization, technology, pace, and the capital markets have all had a major impact on business today, creating the following challenges:

- Shifting channel structures and business relationships — Today's company has morphed into a diversified entity that competes, collaborates, and co-creates in a network of other companies. These entities strive to become virtual organizations. They are forging new relationships, enhancing their supply chains, increasing organizational responsiveness and focusing on bottom line results. Ultimately, those who truly understand how to nurture partnerships, such as relationships with their external suppliers and service providers, will triumph. This is the challenge of business relationships and shifting channel structures;
- Customer satisfaction — Customization, customer value, customer control, customer relationship management, and customer-centric thinking are increasingly being used to describe business focus. This requires companies to divest themselves of self-interest and concentrate on the needs, expectations, and perceptions of those who buy and use their products. What happens when customers' thoughts, wants, and needs drive innovation and flow of goods and services from raw materials suppliers to retailers and ultimately back to those customers? You have customer satisfaction. These requirements are not to be taken lightly; they require a great deal of effort and intense cooperation;
- Speeding time to market — Today's business environment demands speed and more speed. The key to increasing speed to market is the creation of multilevel networks with a view to reducing customer lead-time, production lead-time, and manufacturing lead-time. These net-

works are complex, created through partnerships with suppliers, outsourcing providers, and third parties. They must be flexible, meeting all customer satisfaction requirements through robust design methods enabled by real-time decision tools and manufacturing and distribution synthesis. The networks must be built carefully, with the correct balance of insourcing and outsourcing;
- Information technology — With information technology, companies can extend their market reach and accomplish things beyond the scope of imagination. However, they can also make costly mistakes if they do not use it wisely or properly. It's important to remember that IT will not solve a company's ills by itself, but instead is a critical tool to be applied judiciously so that it facilitates communication between different groups and companies;
- Globalization — New trade agreements, individual countries partnering with each other to produce and export goods, international e-commerce, and Web applications have created a 24/7, on-demand, global marketplace. Politics and technology took us down this path, but the current focus on reducing costs and increasing profits has cemented it into a requirement for doing business today. To answer the challenge of globalization, companies must be aware of when to take advantage of what it has to offer and to think carefully about its impacts on customer satisfaction;
- Virtual factories — Virtual factories are the product of focused factories, deverticalization, the ease of sharing information all over the world, the Web, outsourcing, globalization, and the demand for increasing speed to market. The transformation of huge, outdated manufacturing monoliths into these sleek, lean, flexible, and agile operations presents a major challenge.

- Outsourcing — Today's most unique business challenge is outsourcing because it is both a solution to other business challenges and a challenge in its own right. Numerous companies have had considerable success with outsourcing secondary non-core functions (audit, landscaping, payroll, food services, janitorial, etc.), and so a logical extension is to pursue primary non-core functions (logistics, information technology, marketing, manufacturing, etc.). For outsourcing to work, a solid, up-front effort is required to identify the functions to be outsourced, so that the right processes that have the best returns are considered. Once the identification has been completed, then an organization's outsourcing process must be rigorously applied to assure that the potential benefits of outsourcing are achieved. This is the real challenge of outsourcing — making it a core competency so that it truly is a solution for other business challenges. When you do this, outsourcing is no longer a challenge, but an opportunity.

3 The Outsourcing Opportunity

INTRODUCTION

How do you get past the challenges of outsourcing and make the most of the opportunities it presents? Many companies have had considerable success with outsourcing secondary non-core functions, and forward-thinking companies have had even more success outsourcing primary non-core functions — particularly in operations. When approached properly, outsourcing primary non-core operations yields numerous benefits.

The benefits of operations outsourcing include: reduction in distribution and manufacturing services costs; reduction of hourly and management employees; improved accuracy and flexibility; leveraging (through collaboration) a network greater than your own; access to world-class technology; improved customer satisfaction; improved quality; reduction in capital investment; and cash inflow. There are other, indirect benefits that are realized after outsourcing has been in place for a while, such as business process improvement, increased performance, and resource development.

This chapter explores why organizations outsource operations. Also, because outsourcing primary non-core operations functions is not without controversy, we look at some key sensitive issues. Then we examine the outsourcing opportunity in terms of payback.

WHY ORGANIZATIONS OUTSOURCE OPERATIONS

In the days when vertical enterprises were the norm, operations functions were handled in-house. At that time, it seemed sensible that if a company manufactured products, it should store and distribute them.

Logistics was seen as something that the company should handle in-house, since it was perceived as advantageous to the organization. Who else but the manufacturer could assure that the product it manufactured would get to its end customer on time and in one piece?

In the past two decades, however, keeping all operations in-house has become a burden. This burden had its beginnings with the proliferation of company mergers and acquisitions of product lines. During mergers, similar product lines were purchased along with the manufacturing and distribution operations. Or, two companies merged that were complementary from a product standpoint but not from an operational standpoint. The result was the creation of top-heavy companies, bulging with operations and associated costs.

Outsourcing operations is a method for battling that bulge successfully. By using contract manufacturers, third-party logistics providers, or a combination of both, companies can streamline production and distribution. Consider a successful company that started out manufacturing sports apparel, such as team uniforms. Over time, that company acquired a sports shoe company, a bathing suit company, and several different sports equipment companies. With these acquisitions came factories and distribution centers, and the company soon had too much overhead in factories and distribution centers to be competitive. Outsourcing distribution would streamline these redundant distribution and manufacturing processes without the capital investment of new facilities.

A focus on cost-cutting is another main reason companies outsource operations. When done well, outsourcing operations does save money. For example, a huge pharmaceutical conglomerate that has decided that its core competencies are R&D and product line extensions (PLEs) can dramatically lower costs by divesting itself of processing plants and outsourcing the manufacture. They can then hire a 3PL to handle distribution of their products.

As globalization continues, supply chains are growing more complex at the same time that increased speed-to-market and consistent, satisfactory customer experiences are becoming more important. Even those companies that were once considered in-house manufacturing and logistics leaders are finding that managing the complexities of a global supply chain can hurt performance and drive up costs. Outsourcing one or both functions to providers that have global supply chain experience and have made global supply chain logistics and manufacturing their core competencies can increase efficiency, improve performance, and strengthen customer relations. These expert providers apply sophisticated analysis, modeling and design techniques to build a logistics network that reduces cycle times and inventory while managing multiple vendors.

> ### Outsourcing Data Management Improves Product Flow
>
> In 2002, ES3, a grocery supply distributor based in Keene, New Hampshire, needed to optimize inbound and outbound transportation and monitor logistics activities between multiple manufacturers, numerous carriers, and a large number of destination retail warehouses from its York, Pennsylvania, distribution center. The facility now serves hundreds of manufacturers and retail warehouses with a similar number of carriers, many of them third-party, moving the goods.
>
> This facility needed to offer a stable platform that all parties could access in order to coordinate shipping and tracking. It found the solution in a Web-based, collaborative logistics platform network for inbound and outbound transportation activities developed and hosted by Elogex, an application service provider (ASP) based in Charlotte, North Carolina. Elogex has similar supply chain platform relationships with The Kroger Company, Safeway, Publix, Hannaford Bros, and Dupont.
>
> Under the Elogex-managed system, ES3 now schedules loads to potential carriers in the network via the platform. If one can't accept it, the system automatically defaults to the next carrier. These carriers can also obtain shipments through their Web portals and learn the specific warehouse bay for delivery without ever having to pick up a telephone. Loads can be one unique product, or a combination of multiple products, depending on the needs of the destination retailer.
>
> Elogex provides ES3 with end-to-end transportation management capabilities from shipment planning through freight payment, including real-time visibility and online appointment scheduling. This system brings suppliers, transporters and retailer distribution centers in closer contact, enabling smoother coordination of product fulfillment.[1]

The business challenges discussed in Chapter 2 require that company structures be flexible — even fluid. Forward-thinking companies view manufacturing and logistics as functions that tether them to older ways of doing business. With this mindset, these companies choose to outsource operations so that they can achieve structures that allow them to remain competitive. However, there are companies that still eye operations outsourcing suspiciously — and in some cases, they have good reason.

WHY SOME COMPANIES DON'T OUTSOURCE OPERATIONS

Some companies think that if they outsource manufacturing and logistics, they may lose control of the product's manufacture and delivery. For example, they may feel that since they are not actually making or shipping the product once they outsource, quality might be lost or the customer will not receive it at the right time. They might also believe that the outsourcer won't understand their customer and supplier base.

Companies uncertain about outsourcing operations also worry about losing their knowledge base. After all, if the company is a more established organization, it could at one time have recruited some of industry's heavy hitters in the fields of logistics, manufacturing, and operations. If these functions are outsourced, then leaders must rely on another company's stars, and what if they aren't as big or don't know as much as their own stars? Company leaders may even feel vulnerable to being held captive by their service provider because once the outsourcing is in place, many of the stars are no longer employed and the expertise and leadership in these areas is gone.

The biggest fear, however, is that their operations outsourcing venture might fail, prompting a customer-service public relations nightmare. The media and World Wide Web are full of stories about outsourcing failures. We read about outsourcing contracts that don't survive a year, or how some companies have been forced to bring work back in-house after deciding to outsource. Anyone who reads these stories is likely to wonder about the outcome of their own outsourcing. They may ask, "How much is lost when outsourcing fails? Do you ever get back, in terms of costs and knowledge, what you lost?" These are all legitimate questions.

Outsourcing is a risky business, and if it isn't done correctly, it can hurt a company. The good news is that this damage doesn't have to become a reality. If you follow the process outlined here and rely on the experience of a company that has made outsourcing its core competency, your outsourcing venture will be a success and you will reap the rewards.

The Benefits of Outsourcing

The benefits of outsourcing can be divided into types. First, there are the direct benefits — those that have an immediate impact. Then, there are the indirect benefits — those that outsourcing has on the processes that have remained in-house.

Direct Benefits of Outsourcing

The direct benefits of outsourcing are those related to reduced costs, decreased cycle times, and customer perception and satisfaction. They include:

- Focus on core competency;
- Reduction in the cost of manufacturing and logistics services;
- Reduction in head count of hourly workers and management;
- Improved accuracy;
- Flexibility and wider range of service;
- Access to global networks and superior technology;
- Improved service;
- Improved quality; and
- Reduced capital investment and increased cash inflow.

Let's take a closer look.

Focus on Core Competency

A company that outsources manufacturing, logistics, or both no longer needs all the resources it has been using to make a product, store it, and get it to the customer. Therefore, the company can redirect these resources to its core functions.

This kind of focus can only improve core functions. For example, if a company has decided that its core competency is product design and engineering, outsourcing the product's manufacture means that the design and engineering can only get better because that is now the company's main focus. Workers will not be spread too thinly, managers will have time to focus more on the design process, and leaders can concentrate on new engineering and design as opposed to manufacturing and distribution. The result is likely to be superior design and, when the product gets to the customer, it will be improved because it will have been manufactured by a company whose sole purpose is to manufacture a product developed by a company that knows design better than anyone else.

Reduction in Cost of Manufacturing and Logistics Services

When a company outsources manufacturing, logistics, or both, it can consolidate operations. It no longer has to maintain factories, distribution centers, or inventory. Therefore, the manufacturing and logistics costs to the company that has outsourced are lower because they are no longer responsible for physical plants and personnel related to these operations functions. Also, the vendor might be providing a shared service, so the company is not paying for under-utilized capacity, which will in turn lower inventory-carrying costs.

The notebook (or laptop) computer is an excellent example of how outsourcing manufacturing can reduce costs. At one time, Toshiba dominated the notebook market. When Dell and HP decided to challenge Toshiba, both companies outsourced the manufacturing to Singapore companies. This resulted in lower manufacturing costs, and the two computer giants were able to pass these lower prices on to consumers. Now, Toshiba trails Dell and HP and has outsourced its low-end notebook production to another computer equipment manufacturer in Singapore in an attempt to regain market share.

Contracting Out: Outsourcing Strategies for Medical OEMs

Medical device original equipment manufacturers (OEMs) are outsourcing design and manufacturing more than ever before. Large companies are now strategically contracting out various operations, and both start-ups and the new "virtual companies" are following in their footsteps.

According to Uday Karmarkar, a professor at The Anderson School of Management at the University of California, Los Angeles (UCLA), these companies are critically examining their in-house activities and saying, "We don't have time to do all this [manufacturing] stuff. So let [contract manufacturers] do it, and do it well." Karmarkar also says that an economy of scale always tilts in the OEM's favor when the company removes an operation from its business and contracts with another firm to do it more efficiently.

In addition to admitting that they lack a manufacturing or design competency, and using that admission as the basis for contracting out, OEMs also admit that they can benefit from the years of experience contractors have collected in their niche industries. Contractors specialize in everything from metal-tube fabrication to ergonomic product design. Bill Gaffney, vice president of marketing and international sales at UTI, says of his contract manufacturing company, "We have the experience, the capital equipment, and the technology to do [a particular type of manufacturing] in a very short period of time, as opposed to an OEM trying to develop a manufacturing competency in-house from scratch, which would take a great deal of time."[2]

Reduction in Hourly Worker and Management Head Count
The kind of streamlined, lean company that succeeds in today's marketplace must do so with fewer employees than the companies of the last generation. This is a hard fact for many workers to swallow — whether they are order pickers, plant supervisors, or production managers. But it is true. Downsizing, mergers, acquisitions, and elimination of product lines will not go away.

Outsourcing operations is one of the most effective methods for reducing head count. Instead of reducing head count with a mandate that each department cut 2.5 employees while keeping workload constant (or in many cases, increasing it) entire departments are cut along with the work-load. This means departments that will maintain and grow a company's core competencies do not lose valuable personnel or have more respon-sibilities due to increased workload. In return, the personnel used by outsourcers are trained professionals, many of whom are stars in their respective functions because if they were not, they would cease to be effective service providers. In some cases, outsource providers will even hire workers from the companies that engaged them. This becomes a benefit for the workers because now they are the stars in a company whose core competency is their profession, giving them greater oppor-tunities for growth.

Improved Accuracy

Imagine a busy Saturday at your house. You have a long "to do" list, which includes picking up the dry cleaning, mowing the lawn, buying snacks and drinks to hand out to your child's soccer team after the game, and doing your taxes. While you are shopping, your mind is in a hundred places at once and when you get home, you find that you did not buy enough drinks for the soccer team. Now, suppose you hired a neighbor-hood teen to mow the lawn, asked your spouse to pick up the dry clean-ing, and put your taxes in the hand of a paid accountant before you went shopping. You would probably get the right amount of drinks because you were able to focus on the core task of shopping and did not even think about completing the other tasks.

Now, suppose you have taken a look at your household and realized that there is more at stake than a quiet Saturday or a few drinks at a soc-cer game. After talking things over with your spouse, you decide to hire a nanny. Now, drinks are no longer an issue because you have a nanny to handle those kinds of chores. This allows you to concentrate on other household matters, and you can do a better job with them.

Although these are simple analogies, imagine the impact this scenario has in a more complex environment. When someone (either inside or outside a company) only has to perform one task, it is likely that if that task involves a count or payouts, the completed task will be more accu-rate. If all you have to do is inventory, then your inventory count is more likely to be accurate than if you also have to supervise several plants, pay department bills, maintain a global network of distribution centers, and so on.

Flexibility and Wider Range of Service

If you think that focusing on a core competency and outsourcing the rest is limiting your company, you might want to think again. If you outsource non-core functions, be they primary or secondary, your company has no limits. Let's revisit the busy Saturday scenario. If you have others helping you tackle your "to do" list, there are fewer limits on your time and energy. For example, you can plant bushes or trees in your front yard because someone else has mowed the lawn, and it's not your responsibility. Or, you can hire a landscaper to do the planting, and then you're offering more to your family and neighborhood.

Think of what you can accomplish if you apply your Saturday strategies to your company! You can offer your customers more because, although the company may actually be doing less within its four physical walls, it is accomplishing much more. Your company can produce more, ship greater amounts, and break into product lines heretofore not considered because everything is not being done in-house.

Access to Global Networks and Superior Technology

Contract manufacturers and 3PLs are certainly not new. Many have been doing what they do best for decades. As they have acquired more clients and become more established, contract manufacturers and 3PLs have built sophisticated relationships. Many also belong to multilevel networks that are so necessary for remaining competitive and winning in an established global marketplace. They are also using the superior technology associated with world-class manufacturing and distribution operations, including warehouse management systems (WMSs), transportation management systems (TMSs), manufacturing execution systems (MESs), and operations management systems (OMSs). When a company hires one of these providers, it has the opportunity to access their multilevel logistics networks and use their technology.

During the years of the e-business boom, software vendors like Descartes and Nistevo began linking carriers, suppliers, and purchasers in collaborative networks that have continued to grow even after the dot-com bust. A number of outsourcing providers are plugged into these networks, and that puts them at the disposal of any company that engages them. Contract electronics manufacturers like Flextronics and Solectron also have access to networks, and now these networks are part of their offerings to customers.

Using outsourcers such as these organizations means that a company does not have to build complex networks on its own. Smaller operations can share space, as well as IT support and operations, and all companies can leverage provider networks to consolidate loads. For example, the largest 3PLs support regional cross-docks in far more areas than any one company does. This broader network offers the opportunity to consolidate shipments more efficiently to reduce transportation costs.[3]

Outsourcing Fleet Management Moves Furniture Around the World

William Harris no longer has to wake up at 2:00 a.m. to handle emergency phone calls about flat tires. That's because Harris, director of transportation for Henredon Furniture, has outsourced all transportation and fleet management.

Henredon, a subsidiary of Lifestyle Furnishings International Ltd., produces high-end dining, bedroom and living room furniture. After four decades of fleet ownership, Henredon considered outsourcing for the first time in the late 1980s. So, the company started small, leasing 14 tractors and 32 trailers.

The logistics provider then began operating Henredon's shop, including preventive maintenance, DOT/EPA regulations, vehicle substitution, washing, permitting, tires, parts, road service, tags, and tax reporting. Recently, they added an on-site dispatching center that handles route coordination throughout all 30 states serviced by Henredon.

Freedom from vehicle maintenance is a huge benefit of outsourcing, says Harris. Another is the ability to take advantage of their provider's purchasing power. "They get much more reasonable rates, not only for original vehicles but also for maintenance items and repair parts, than we ever could," says Harris.

The partnership between the companies is working out for the long term, says Harris. First, Henredon has increased the size of the fleet to 25 tractors and 75 trailers. Second, Harris can choose to rent more vehicles during peak periods like Thanksgiving and Christmas, on an as-needed basis.

All in all, outsourcing helps Henredon meet a number of crucial business and transportation challenges, says Harris. First, furniture keeps getting bigger and heavier. Second, back hauling, where the return trip of a delivery truck is used to move furniture, is commonplace. Third, the growing popularity of Henredon products has created a more complex supply chain.

In addition, customers who are retail dealers are demanding shorter delivery cycles.

Because Henredon practices outsourcing, they can guarantee delivery to retailers. "That is an important Henredon strategy," Harris adds. "That's why the fleet has to be well maintained — to meet the commitment to our dealers, on time and damage free."

Harris is confident that the growth and challenges are manageable by relying on and fortifying one of the company's greatest assets: Its drivers. "Out of 22 drivers, we have three sets of brothers, as well as two sons of former Henredon drivers," Harris says. "They are a part of the Henredon family."[4]

Improved Service

Outsourcing manufacturing and logistics improves service by shortening cycle times and speeding time to market. Tapping into capabilities not available internally increases scheduling flexibility and resource availability, which usually results in reduced time to market. BMW, for instance, wanted to bring its lower priced X3 SUV to market quicker, so the company outsourced its manufacture to Magna Steyr, an Austrian carmaker.[5]

3PLs receive and store raw material or finished inventory, consume inventory in the production process, produce finished goods, and ship finished goods to customers — all the while maintaining inventory. So, improved inventory visibility and accountability, as well as on-time delivery, are all part of their packages. This ensures higher levels of customer satisfaction.

Improved Quality

It's interesting: many companies that have already outsourced manufacturing, logistics, or both originally did so to cut costs. However, they have now found that not only can outsourcing reduce overhead, it can also improve quality. This quality improvement is due to the fact that outsourcing providers running volume operations have better quality assurance (QA) programs in place than the average company that is still trying to do it in-house. According to Gary Koh, CEO and managing director of Genesis Advanced Technologies, "Their critical mass in a particular discipline allows them to develop reliable processes including quality control."[6] The results are less damage, less rework, improved response time to inquiries, and greater inventory accuracy.

Reduced Capital Investment and Increased Cash Inflow

Outsourcing manufacturing, logistics, or both will reduce capital investment. This is because once these processes are contracted out, the facilities previously used by the company are removed from the balance sheet. If you no longer make or assemble your product, then you no longer need to maintain factories. If you have outsourced distribution, then you no longer need distribution centers or warehouses. This makes capital funds more available for a company's core functions. Outsourcing can also eliminate the need to demonstrate return on equity from capital investments in non-core areas, and this can improve certain financial measurements.

So, what do companies do with assets they no longer need? They sell them. Equipment, facilities, vehicles and licenses used in current operations all have a value. Often, companies can sell them to the outsource provider at book rather than market value, or they may find a market for them elsewhere. But whether they sell unneeded assets to the provider or to another party, companies still end up with an infusion of cash, either because they don't have the expense of maintaining the facilities or equipment or they sold them.

The Indirect Benefits of Outsourcing

A company that decides to outsource operations functions often finds that its internal processes benefit from the decision. These are benefits that aren't as obvious as the direct ones because they subtly affect a company's bottom line. Indirect benefits include:

- Creating a catalyst for change — In the search for core competencies, how outsourced operations are managed is highlighted. Companies can take a closer look at engineered operations, planning, and scheduling. The result is a better grasp of accountability and root cause analysis, which can only improve core functions;
- Initiating or fueling change — A company is often able to offer new services and capabilities because outsourcing has increased performance in the form of shorter lead times and reduction in the landed cost to the customer;
- Stimulating analysis — The requirement to document business processes (and their costs) inherent with any outsourcing implementation often uncovers valuable information that can be studied and put to use within the organization. In other words, developing metrics to use to select a third-party provider may result in asking why these metrics aren't used throughout the company;
- Converting sluggish functional areas into dynamic ones — The actual process of finding a provider and performing a baseline analysis will cause a company to look internally to improve processes. This often breathes new life into functions such as customer service, purchasing, and procurement; and
- Resource and contact development — After a successful outsourcing implementation, companies often find they have access to new business resources and personnel, such as freight handlers, value-added service providers, and IT. Using these contacts, they can form new and beneficial relationships.

When direct and indirect benefits of outsourcing are laid out, it's easy to see why so many companies are already outsourcing or planning to do so. A company that outsources operations has much to gain. Yes, there are risks. Yes, it is possible that an outsourcing strategy will fail. But if you know how to approach outsourcing or work with experts who have made outsourcing a core competency, the benefits far outweigh the risks. The key to the outsourcing opportunity is in your strategy — defining your core competencies, defining targets, and managing your outsourcing relationships. Upcoming chapters will address these issues.

---

1 Gary N. Bowen, "Outsourcing Collaborative Logistics Empowers Retail Supply Chain Managers," *Outsourcing Journal*, July 2003. http://www.outsourcing-supply-chain-management.com/logisitics.html

2 Maureen Kingsley. "Contracting Out: Outsourcing Strategies for Medical OEMs." *Medical Devicelink.com*, November 11, 2003. http://www.devicelink.com/mddi/archive/03/11/005.html.

3 "Why Outsourcing is Suddenly In," *CNET News.com*, Sept. 29, 2002. http://news.com.com/2009-1001_3-959785.html.

4 "Fleet Management," *Businessweek.com*, http://www.businessweek.com/adsection/outsource/outsourcsfleet.htm.

5 Dan Lienart, "First Look: The New BMW and 6-Series Coupe," *Forbes.com*, October 13, 2003. http://www.forbes.com/2003/10/13/cx_dl_1013feat.html.

6 Gary Koh, "The Leveraged Corporation: Outsourcing to Your Advantage," *BOMA*. 2002-2003. http://www.bomacorp.com/stories/outsourcing.html.

ON THE ELEVATOR

In the days when vertical enterprises were the norm, operations functions were handled in-house. In the past two decades, however, keeping all operations in-house has become a burden. Outsourcing operations is a method that lets someone else carry that burden. By using contract manufacturers, third-party logistics providers, or a combination of both, companies can streamline production and distribution.

There are risks to outsourcing. Stories of failed outsourcing initiatives abound. But, if you know how to approach outsourcing or work with someone who fully understands the outsourcing process and has made it a core competency, the benefits far outweigh the risks. When done properly, outsourcing primary non-core operations functions yields a wealth of benefits — those with direct impact on a company and those that are not as obvious but affect the services that remain in-house. Direct benefits include:

- Focus on core competency;
- Reduction in manufacturing and logistics costs through the consolidation of operations and reduction of inventory carrying and transportation costs;
- Reduction in management and hourly head count;
- Improved accuracy through better inventory visibility and production tracking;
- Flexibility and wider range of service;
- Access to global networks and superior technology (world-class WMS, TMS, MES, OMS) results in the collaboration that consolidates loads, and allows smaller organizations to share space, IT support, and operation;

- Improved service through shorter order cycle time, visibility of available inventory, and accountability;
- Improved quality resulting from less damage, less scrap, and improved response time to inquiries; and
- Reduction in capital investment and increased cash infusion because facilities are no longer on the balance sheet and assets can be sold.

The indirect benefits of operations outsourcing are:

- Creating a catalyst for change by highlighting how outsourced operations are managed;
- Initiating or fueling expansion by allowing a company to offer new services because outsourcing has improved performance;
- Stimulating analysis due to the requirement to document business processes and their costs;
- Converting sluggish functional areas into dynamic, successful ones; and
- Developing resources and contacts brought to the table by the service provider.

The key to taking advantage of all outsourcing has to offer lies in your outsourcing strategy — defining your core competencies, defining targets, and managing your outsourcing relationships. Upcoming chapters address these issues and more.

4 Defining Core

INTRODUCTION

Today's economic climate makes it virtually impossible not to outsource. But to take the plunge into outsourcing without a robust process will not only prevent an organization from achieving the benefits, it will likely result in a major setback. To prevent this, an organization must look deep within itself and identify its core function or functions. And, before the organization can start this important part of the process, it must first understand its goals and have a strategic vision and plan in place.

Goals are what the organization hopes to achieve in the medium- to long-term future. To understand company goals, a company's leaders should ask themselves these key questions:

- Where is the company headed?
- How will we get there?
- What is the science of our business?
- What values will be practiced?
- How will we measure success?

Answering these questions will not only help leaders see the company's goals clearly, but will also help form the framework for defining the company's strategic vision and plan.

By addressing the "where" portion of the goals, leaders can create the company's strategic vision. The vision should be stated such that the present is described as a past condition of the future. As a mental picture of the future, it should be an expression of hope, excellence, ideals, and possibilities for the company. Each vision should be unique and can only be appropriate for that company.

When company leaders work to answer the "how" portion of their company's goals, they are also defining their strategic plan, or mission. This plan serves as the focal point of the company's operating principles. For example, if one of the company's goals is complete customer satisfaction, then how it will achieve that goal then becomes the strategic plan. Will the company follow in the footsteps of Tiffany's, which envisions pampering, gratifying, and entertaining customers as the means of achieving complete customer satisfaction? Or will they emulate Wal-Mart by assuring their customers that they will get friendly and fast service at the best price?[1]

While the organization is working on its strategic vision and mission, it should also define its requirements for success; this is because outsourcing includes its own requirements for success. Therefore, identifying the requirements for success for the whole company sets the stage for establishing the outsourcing requirements for success. A company's requirements for success answer the following questions:

- What is the science of our business?
- What functions are core to our success?
- What functions are required but are not core?

The requirements should also present the basic truths of the company, in the company's own language, so that everyone understands the underpinnings. From there, the company can underscore its values by creating guiding principles and then devise a set of criteria for measuring the company's success.[2]

This up-front legwork may seem daunting, but it is not. In most cases, it takes less than a month, and the benefits, although difficult to measure, are very significant. In the end, you will have a solid strategy upon which to grow your organization's success. This makes it easier for company leaders to view the big picture and truly focus on defining core competency. At the same time, the needs of the company's customers and how the company will meet them will become clearer. This chapter delves deep into the differences between primary and secondary core functions and primary and secondary non-core functions, discusses the process of defining core, and then takes a look at evaluating processes for outsourcing.

CORE VERSUS NON-CORE

Business processes can be divided into two types: core functions and non-core functions. "Core functions" is the answer to the question: What is this business all about? Non-core functions are processes that either add significant value to the core product or service or provide the means for supporting the company and retaining employees (for example, HVAC, security, cleaning, landscaping, payroll, maintenance, and so on). These two types of functions can be further divided into what kind of focus they have: primary or secondary. In other words, there are primary and secondary core functions and primary and secondary non-core functions. This can be illustrated in a simple matrix (Figure 1).

	Primary Focus	Secondary Focus
Core Process	Things that differentiate your organization in the market-place. The reasons customers come to you.	Things that need to be done well but are not visible to the customer.
Non-Core Process	Things that, if not done well, can have a negative impact on your customer relationship.	Things that need to be done but do not have any significant impact on the success of the business.

Figure 1: Core Competency Matrix

Primary core functions are those that differentiate your company from the rest; they are the reasons your customers come to you! Consider a "chic" retailer like Gap. What differentiates them from other companies and brings customers to them? The answers to that question would most likely be their retail stores, their merchandising, their brand, and their relationship (or touch points) with the customer. You can arrive at similar answers for your company by asking, "If I outsource this function, how will it affect my relationship with the customer?"

Identifying core and non-core functions hinges on how you touch your customers. Consider the customer touch points the retailer might have — retail stores, website, package delivery, and customer service. If this retailer outsourced its retail stores to someone else, what would happen with its customers? It might lose them. But, if the retailer outsourced package delivery, it is quite possible that the customer would still purchase products from the company. Primary and secondary core processes, therefore, are customer-centric and must be done well for a company to remain in business, prosper, and grow.

At times, it can be difficult to distinguish secondary core functions from primary core or even primary non-core. Again, how you touch your customers can help you make the distinction. Customer service is a good example: some companies outsource it and some don't. Those who don't outsource customer service have probably decided that customer service is intricately interwoven within their customer's perception of the company—this is the case with a lot of catalog companies and direct marketers. Customer service is one of those functions that really requires some thought. And the more time you spend wondering about it, the more likely it is to be considered a secondary core.

The Importance of Focusing on Core Competencies

In an article in the November 25, 2002 issue of *Fortune* magazine, the author wrote about the challenges pharmaceutical giant Bayer faced while manufacturing its hemophilia drug Kogenate FS.

Developing the drug was easy for Bayer, because the company is a strong drug innovator. However, manufacturing it was more problematic because the company was relatively weak in terms of its own operations and efficiency. As a result, the drug's market potential suffered and patients had to wait longer to receive treatment. Two years ago, FDA inspectors offered a tepid review of Bayer's manufacturing site for this drug.

Bayer took the feedback from the FDA seriously and worked hard to improve its capabilities, and now has a state-of-the-art plant in which to produce the drug. Production levels are reaching healthy conditions again, which is good news for hemophilia patients. However, there is a lesson here: If Bayer had concentrated solely on its R&D strength and outsourced its manufacturing, the company might not have missed a beat at all.

By contrast, biotech company Amgen, the maker of Epogen and Neupogen, focuses on its core competency, R&D, managing to achieve success through sales of just a few core drugs. Amgen executives also think ahead: They started developing new drugs back in the mid-1990s to replace drugs that were about to reach the end of their lifecycle. This was a natural next step for Amgen at the time, since its focus was on drug development. Doing what it does best has helped Amgen receive optimal results.[3]

Primary non-core processes are those non-core processes that add significant value to your product or service — and they are also noticed by customers. If these processes are not done well, they will have a negative impact on your bottom line, although they might not put you out of business altogether. For the retailer, the primary non-core functions could be IT, HR, and logistics.

Secondary non-core functions are those that do not really affect your revenues. They are distinguished from primary and secondary core functions and primary non-core functions by one important difference — your customers do not drive them. Secondary non-core functions include payroll, landscaping, food service, security, and maintenance. Most companies have many of the same non-core functions, but there are some that are specific to the company such as store supplies for the retailer and printing for the publisher.

To help make the distinctions in your company's core competencies, you can take the below matrix and apply it to your company. For the retailer, the matrix might look like this:

	Primary Focus	Secondary Focus
Core Process	• Retail Stores • Merchandising • Brand	• Procurement • Sourcing • Real Estate
Non-Core Process	• IT • HR • Logistics	• Store Supplies • Accounting • Landscaping

Figure 2: Core Competency Matrix for the Chic Retailer

When the core and non-core competencies are presented like this, it makes it simpler to think about what to keep in-house and what to outsource. Here is the matrix again (Figure 3), but this time applied to a manufacturing/distribution company:

	Primary Focus	Secondary Focus
Core Process	• Production • Product Design • Production Planning and Scheduling	• Procurement • Logistics • HR • Maintenance
Non-Core Process	• IT • Finance and Accounting • Sales and Marketing	• Real Estate • Food Service • Landscaping

Figure 3: Core Competency Matrix for a Manufacturer/Distributor

As you can see in Figure 3, the company's core processes are production, product design, production planning and scheduling, procurement, logistics, HR, and maintenance. The company could likely keep all of these functions in-house, but it might not be as profitable as it would if it decided to outsource maintenance and HR. Also, the company could decide that since sales and marketing are non-core, these functions could be outsourced; however, that might negatively impact the customer's perception of the company.

Why is defining primary and secondary core and non-core competencies so important? The answer to that question is simple: because once these distinctions are made, company leaders can spend their time focusing on what is important to the company's customers and what will add the most to the company's success. Currently, corporate leaders do not have enough hours in the day to do all that needs to be done. And, when they sit down and look at what they're spending their time on, they see that much of that time is spent dealing with issues that do not necessarily drive the company's success.

For example, think about how much time is spent gathering and analyzing data before a company sees the result and can take action. Suppose a company looked at its processes and determined that data analysis is not what it does best. So, they found someone else to mine data, analyze it, and provide company leaders with a report full of all the information they need to make informed decisions about their business. The result is that these leaders had much more time to focus on what truly drives their business.

Consider NASA. It was founded to run space programs, but over the years, it added such functions as telemetry and tracking facilities to its business activities. These activities consumed a great deal of NASA's time and yet were not really NASA's bailiwick. Imagine the effect on your tax dollars. Now, they outsource these activities and have returned to their core business activity — the thing they do best, which is running U.S. space programs.

As you can see, it is critical to define core competencies and then to subdivide them into primary and secondary core, continually asking how each function touches your customer. Once that is accomplished, you will have a better picture of what functions you should outsource. So, how do you set about doing this? It can be accomplished through teamwork, by dividing your company into its different business processes, and asking questions about each process.

IDENTIFYING CORE TAKES TEAMWORK

The first step in defining core and non-core is to create a team comprised of company leaders and managers that is dedicated to defining core and non-core functions and deciding how much time is spent on each. The team will also be charged with taking this information and deciding what secondary core and non-core functions could be outsourced. Team members must understand the strategic nature of the company's vision and be involved in all aspects of the company. They must also be able to evaluate the company's strengths, weaknesses, and opportunities. The leader of this team must be a well-organized, action-based leader (in most cases, the company's CEO) with a broad-based perspective and a strong belief in the collaboration process. The team leader will ensure quality communications and participation, manage meetings, and provide focus on the task of defining core functions.

Who should make up this vital team? A member from each of the areas defined as main operating functions should be included on the team, typically about seven to ten people representing a cross-section of the entire organization. The team should spend about four to six weeks deciding how much time is currently being spent on each function and whether that is the amount of time that should be spent. With this process, the team should not look at the past, but instead focus on the future. Company leaders need to be part of this process to ensure buy-in as outsourcing candidates are identified.

After the team has gone through the process above and has created a core competency matrix like those illustrated, a re-evaluation process begins. For example, if there is a function that takes up company time that team members believe should have *even more time* devoted to it, that process may be identified as a primary core function that should not be outsourced. The converse may be true in other situations. If the company is spending a great deal of time on logistics that would be better spent on product innovation, then logistics could be considered a primary non-core function that can be outsourced.

DIVIDE AND CONQUER

The next step that the core-defining team must take is breaking down operations into discrete processes, based on the company's relationship with the customer, the product(s) it provides, and the services that support getting that product to the end customer. This step is necessary whether the product is a durable good, brand, specialized service, or something else. One way to succeed at this step is to consider the company's relationship with the customer and how the customer perceives the company, the product(s), and the effort and materials that go into making it. Then break down the services that support making the product(s), which might include production, IT, administration, logistics, security, and marketing/advertising. Another way to approach this is to list the company's capabilities and then assign them to appropriate business processes.

The objective here is to make the identification of core competency less daunting. Breaking a company into manageable chunks allows the team to focus on all aspects of the business. This breaking-down task also promotes awareness of exactly what goes on in the company and of what might actually be successful if it were done outside the company.

In many ways, this task is a brainstorming session, and the team does not have to get this precisely right at first. As the team goes through the action of critically evaluating business processes and support services, these business processes will be further defined and might be either consolidated or subdivided, depending on availability of service providers on the outside. A simple example of this is a company that lists distribution and transportation as separate business processes. Later, this company realizes that there is so much overlap between the two that the process may actually be logistics. Or, a company may list production as one of its business processes and then realize that production can be further divided into innovation, design, and manufacturing. Once this task is complete, the discussion of which business processes are core and which are non-core can begin.

QUESTIONS AND ANSWERS

Now that the team has divided the company into business processes, a set of questions can be asked to determine its core processes. At this point, the team is not deciding which are primary core processes and which are secondary core processes, but instead is determining its *overall core competencies*. These questions include:

- Who are our customers?
- How do the functions we have defined touch the customer? Or do they touch the customer?
- What is it that our customers know us for most?

- What is it that our company does that provides the most value to the customer?
- What is it that we do that may be difficult for our competitors to imitate?

As the team answers these questions, an idea of the company's primary competencies will begin to take shape. However, the team should be mindful that what may first seem to be critical to the company's success may actually not be, and that is why the third question is extremely important. For example, a team defining core for Starbucks might say that coffee is what its customers know it for best, and serving a variety of coffee drinks made to customers' specifications provides the most value to the customer. But a number of companies are known for their coffee (think "Folgers"), and there are other coffee houses that serve a variety of made-to-order coffee drinks.

So, what is it that Starbucks is truly known for? Its brand. Say the name "Starbucks" and just about anyone listening will see the Starbucks logo and picture the Starbucks located closest to them. Starbucks capitalizes on that brand recognition, using it to penetrate markets and boost sales.

The next set of questions to ask can help ensure that the team is truly honing in on defining core business processes:

- Is there a service around what we believe is our core that contributes a great deal of value or exceeds the value of our primary product? Is it customer service? Delivery service? Value-added service?
- Would our primary product be the same if we didn't provide these services?
- Do our customers see this service as an important differentiator?

Answering these questions will help determine whether or not your company is better at making a product or servicing it. Suppose you are part of the core defining team at Domino's. Does Domino's make the best pizza on the market? Some people might think so, but the answer likely is "No." Is Domino's pizza the cheapest? No. So, what does Domino's do best? They can make a pizza in less than 8 minutes and deliver it in 45 minutes or less. If Domino's ever had to choose between making pizza that is featured in *Gourmet* magazine or making pizza fast and delivering it, we would hope that it would choose the latter. In fact, Domino's could offer this service to other pizza makers with better recipes who want to re-engineer the pizza making process for faster service. A similar distinction could be made for a printing company that also does order fulfillment. The company's defining core team could look at its warehousing and distribution functions and realize that its product — printed materials — is not as important to customers as those functions. That company may then realize that its core competency is fulfillment and not printing.

Service over Product: Three-Five Systems

In 2000, Three-Five Systems was a high-flying technology company that sold cell-phone displays to Motorola. These sales represented as much as 80% of the company's revenue at the time. When the dot-com bubble burst, Three-Five Systems crashed along with the cell-phone business. But with the help of a few acquisitions in the past two years and a re-evaluation of its core competency, which was not the displays themselves but display technology, the company has morphed into a more diversified provider of electronic manufacturing services (EMS).

"Their whole strategy is to become a specialty electronic manufacturing service company, leveraging their core competency in display technology," says Graham Tanaka of the Tanaka Growth Fund. "I think it is a good move." The company still has a focus on displays and is aiming to build its business into two areas that may provide the lion's share of profit growth, since these areas produce higher profit margins than those earned by the typical EMS company. First, casinos are interested in putting displays on gambling devices such as slot machines to track and communicate with high rollers when they swipe their smart cards. Second, Three-Five Systems is getting U.S. Food and Drug Administration approval to make medical equipment used in life and death situations, known as "Class III" medical devices.[4]

The core-defining team can further determine whether a physical product or a service is core by asking:

- What percentage of the cost of goods sold do these services make up?
- Do these services and the way they support our primary product align with future goals for our organization?
- Would the individuals running these services ever run our company?
- Does/could the business they perform exist outside of our company? Is there an example of one outside of our company?

Your core-defining team must be prepared to face some possibly difficult facts as they answer these questions. If you see that the services supporting your product are eating into your profits and yet are not being done as well as they should, then perhaps they are not core functions, even if your company has been supporting those services for generations. If your company's goal is to manufacture the best motherboards in the PC industry, perhaps delivering those motherboards to the PC faster than anyone else in the world is not aligned with that goal.

Probably the most difficult of all the questions involves looking at who runs the business and identifying their contributions to the organization. A good exercise to go through is to take the company organizational chart and look at the leader of each operation, asking "Could this person be CEO of this company one day?" Put a "Yes" or "No" by their names, remembering that the answer should be based on *that leader's function* and *not the leader's personal credentials.* If the answer is "Yes," that area is a candidate for primary core, and if the answer is "No," then that may be a non-core function that can be outsourced. In the case of secondary core, the exercise of separating primary and secondary core functions is a little more difficult. The question to ask here is what kind of risk do we run outsourcing this function?

The next step is to take the non-core functions identified and determine if there is an outside company that has these functions as its primary core. If the answer is "Yes" then that function is defined as a non-core function that could be outsourced.

Answering all the questions listed above for each business process will not be easy. But in the end, the team will have identified the organization's core competencies, as well as its non-core functions. At this point, your core-defining team can begin the process of identifying primary core competencies and secondary core competencies.

This is where your answer or answers to "What does our customer know us for most and how do we best touch the customer?" are all-important. Perhaps your customer knows you mainly for your brand. Or maybe your customers recognize your company as the one that developed a life-saving drug or made it easier for you to ship packages. Your primary core competencies are going to be those your customer perceives as differentiating you from your competitors.

Your secondary core competencies are more likely to be found in the answer to the question, "What do we do that brings the most value to the customer?" In other words, your customers may not know everything you do to make their experiences all they expect or more, but if these things are not done well, you will lose them. Imagine a customer's reaction if the motherboard died on a Dell computer he had purchased a few days earlier. Customers rarely say, "Yeah, I buy Dell computers because their motherboards are the best in the business," but if all of a sudden Dell motherboards crashed within days of a purchase, Dell wouldn't be in business much longer. You may also want to ask yourself, "What do I risk if I try to outsource this function?" If you determine that there is a small risk, but that it is worth taking for the sake of improving other functions, then you have most likely identified a secondary core function.

Identifying primary and secondary core functions is critical to deciding which functions to keep in-house and which to outsource. Some may think that this decision is a no-brainer. Surely, only non-core functions should be outsourced while all core functions should be kept in-house, right? Not necessarily! A company may be able to compete better in the marketplace if it outsources a secondary core function or if it keeps a primary non-core function in-house. That is why the distinctions between primary core and secondary core are so crucial. Once you have made these distinctions, you are ready to begin the process of evaluating functions and reaching a consensus about which processes will be kept in-house and which will be done by other organizations.

BEGINNING THE EVALUATION PROCESS

Before you begin the evaluation process, realize that this can be even more difficult than defining core because word will soon be out that functions will be outsourced. People are likely to become secretive and resentful because they are fear losing their jobs. While being laid off is only one of the three staffing outcomes of outsourcing — the other two are transfers to the service provider and redeployment elsewhere in the organization — layoffs after outsourcing get the most press. And Corporate America doesn't help. An article in *USA Today* in April of 2004 reported that in some companies, American employees losing their jobs to India had to train their replacements before leaving the company. Therefore, it cannot be stressed enough how crucial it is to have correct, consistent, and timely communication with the right people within the company. Keeping staff informed through regular communication and monitoring overall morale goes a long way toward easing fear, doubt, and uncertainty as you begin the task of evaluating business processes.

The first step in evaluating business processes for outsourcing is identifying which processes need strategic outsourcing and which should be contracted. Strategic outsourcing, which is what is meant here by "outsourcing," involves working with one or more service providers in order to effect a significant improvement in business performance. Strategic outsourcing is best suited to secondary core and primary non-core functions, although there may be a few primary non-core functions that can be contracted or a secondary non-core process that should be strategically outsourced. And strategic outsourcing is only likely to bring the desired results if management is prepared to adopt a completely new perspective on management control. The Core Competency Matrix can help you in this process (Figure 4).

	Primary Focus	Secondary Focus
Core Process	• Insource	• Insource • Outsource
Non-Core Process	• Insource • Outsource • Contract	• Outsource • Contract

Figure 4: Core Competency Matrix

Strategic Outsourcing: Nike

Nike sells more than 40 million pairs of running shoes each year, yet it does not manufacture any of them. Instead, Nike uses a worldwide network of outsourcers for its manufacturing. Nike refers to those companies that have been its long-time suppliers of its most expensive products as "Developed Partners." These suppliers have the knowledge, technology, and expertise to produce those products Nike is best known for — the shoes worn by NBA teams, for example. In other words, these suppliers are close to the core of Nike's business.

Nike's production network is not static, and its head office is constantly redefining its supplier system. Many of its Developed Partners are created from companies that Nike has gradually upgraded by assigning experienced technicians to train semi-skilled workers. Nike's relationship with its suppliers is usually credited as the source of its competitive advantage — they truly are partners and not contractors.[5]

Strategic outsourcing is quite different from contracting. Contracting basically delegates the responsibility to an organization and then lets them get on with it. The contractor involved will have no real interest in the purchasing organization once is own responsibilities have been fulfilled. Hiring a landscaper to take care of a company's grounds is a very good example of a secondary non-core function that is best suited to contracting (although there can be secondary non-core functions that warrant strategic outsourcing).

Making these determinations is critical in understanding the possible benefits from outsourcing. From this point, you can develop a baseline for objective decision-making, define the businesses processes and their value, and recognize what non-core functions contribute to your business and which functions simply help support your physical plant and employees.

1 Jim Tompkins. *Revolution: Take Charge Strategies for Business Success.* Raleigh, NC,1998, pp. 61-62.

2 Tompkins, *Revolution,* pp. 63, 67.

3 Brian Roberts. "Bayer, Amgen Refocus Their Core Competencies." *Inside 1to1,* January 6, 2003, http://www.1to1.com/View.aspx?DocID=25492.

4 Michael Brush. "4 Tech Insiders Are Buying." *MSN Money,* May 26, 2004 http://moneycentral.msn.com/content/P81686.asp

5 Simon Domberger. *The Contracting Organization: A Strategic Guide to Outsourcing,* London: 1998, p. 129.

ON THE ELEVATOR

Before beginning the important process of defining core processes, you must understand your company's goals and have a strategic vision and plan in place. To grasp company goals, leaders should ask themselves these questions:

- Where is the company headed?
- How will we get there?
- What is the science of our business?
- What values will be practiced?
- How will we measure success?

By addressing the "Where" portion of the goals, leaders can create the company's strategic vision. When company leaders work to answer the "How" portion of their company's goals, they are also defining the company's strategic plan, or mission. Completing these tasks makes it easier for company leaders to step back, evaluate the results, and then set about defining the company's core competency.

The process of defining "Core" requires awareness of the four types of business functions within a company — primary core, secondary core, primary non-core, and secondary non-core. Primary core functions are the things that differentiate your company in the marketplace, and more importantly, they are the reasons your customers come to you. Secondary core functions are those things that bring value to your customer and must be done well, but at the same time, they are not visible to your customer. Primary non-core functions are those that can affect your relationship with your customer but are not what your business is about. Secondary non-core functions are those processes that

are necessary for running the business but do not affect your company's success.

To properly define "core," develop a team made up of company leaders who understand the strategic nature of the vision. Breaking the company up into discrete processes is one of the first tasks this group must undertake. These discrete processes will become more defined further down the road and may be consolidated or divided even further, depending on the availability of external service providers. This task helps break down the decision into manageable chunks.

Once this process is complete, the discussion of defining "core" can begin. There are some definite questions that must be asked in order to understand and evaluate "core." These questions are:

- Who are our customers?
- How do the functions we have defined touch the customer? Or do they touch the customer?
- What is it that our customers know us for most?
- What is it that our company does that provides the most value to the customer?
- What is it that we do that may be difficult for our competitors to imitate?

Answering all of these questions for each of the business processes you have defined will help you understand if they are core functions. Once you have defined "core" and its supporting processes, there needs to be consensus around which functions to evaluate for outsourcing.

5 Defining Outsourcing Targets

INTRODUCTION

Chapter 4 covered the process of defining core competencies once management has made the general decision to outsource selected functions or operations. And once you have defined your primary core processes, you will have a list of other functions and activities — some of which may be immediately recognized as possible outsourcing targets and others that may need further evaluation. Now it is time to take this important list and evaluate it, searching for areas where outsourcing will have the most value and defining other areas where more detail is needed.

Determining the functions and segments where outsourcing will have the most value is a critical part of the outsourcing process; however, the wrong factors are often used to make this decision. Currently, most outsourcing decisions are based on the economic returns or savings compared to the cost, when the real reason companies should outsource is the need to focus management time and resources on what is most critical. It is true that cost savings and service improvements are gained from outsourcing, but these are actually only side benefits. The real driver behind outsourcing must be management focus.

A look at almost any organization's history shows the deterioration in performance that occurs when company leaders and management "take their eyes off the ball" and begin to focus on non-core activities. Eventually, their profit performance declines and their competitiveness weakens. Companies must focus management time and attention on their core competencies and maintain efforts to continuously improve them. If company leaders do not focus on core functions, they will soon fall into the valley that follows peak performance.

Core Competency Focus: NCI Vehicle Rescue

Think of the British equivalent of AAA combined with an insurance company, and you will have an idea of what NCI Vehicle Rescue is about, except that so far it is a bit smaller and doesn't directly employ most of the people who represent the operation.

In a typical 21st century operation, virtually every aspect of the business is outsourced, from the call center that acts as the first line of contact, to the local mechanics that come to fix or tow away damaged vehicles. This leaves NCI free to focus on selling breakdown coverage, but keeps overhead low, the benefits of which can be passed on to customers.

The breakdown coverage sold by NCI is a fully-insured product backed by Groupama, and a network of 'independent recovery agents' (local mechanics) throughout the UK and Europe. NCI only has to pay them when they are called out for assistance, and it does not have to build its own fleet of vehicles or employ technicians that are available 24/7.

Each NCI policy sold carries full insurance against call-out charges, so the company has no exposure to claims. The company currently has more than 10,000 vehicles on its books and the number is climbing.[1]

The natural order of life is peak-to-valley-to-peak-to-valley. Today, the only way to circumvent this and achieve continuous peak performance is to chip away at those functions that prevent company leaders and managers from focusing on core. For a company to enjoy peak performance, leaders ought to spend 60-80% of their time focusing on primary core functions, 10-30% on secondary core functions, 10% on primary non-core functions and 0% on secondary non-core functions. That same company's managers will see their time split a little more evenly on the core functions with 40% spent on both primary and secondary core functions, 20% on primary non-core function, and 0% on secondary functions. Once a company slips below these numbers for its leaders, managers or both, it won't be long until leaders are only spending 20% of their time on primary core and managers are not spending any time on primary. This scenario will put the company right in the heart of the valley, and perhaps unable to climb back up. All this can be summarized in two matrices similar to those discussed in the previous chapter (Figures 1 and 2).

	Core Process		Non-Core Process	
	Primary	Secondary	Primary	Secondary
Peak Performance	80%	10%	10%	0%
Valley Performance	20%	30%	30%	20%

Figure 1: How Leadership Focus Results in Peak-to-Valley Performance

	Core Process		Non-Core Process	
	Primary	Secondary	Primary	Secondary
Peak Performance	40%	40%	20%	0%
Valley Performance	0%	40%	40%	20%

Figure 2: How Management Focus Results in Peak-to-Valley Performance

Therefore, functions that are outside of the primary core (and that can include secondary core) should be outsourced to free management time and organizational resources so that the company can work on the highest priority activities — primary core competencies. Yes, even secondary core activities are candidates for outsourcing. For example, a company may determine, without ambiguity, that its core competencies are manufacturing both gears and widgets and that it exceeds its competitors in the sales of both. Proponents of the notion that you must not outsource any core competencies would not consider outsourcing the manufacture of either product. However, if a persistent outsourcing team continues to drill down, it may learn that while the company dominates the market for both products, it is really stronger in the widget market. Therefore, a wise decision might be to outsource gear production.

The widget and gear manufacturer is an excellent example of how a company should not rush headlong into an outsourcing strategy without careful evaluation and analysis. A company should learn about internal process needs and service requirements for the functions or processes, and it must also understand the cost structure of the functions or processes that are candidates for outsourcing; otherwise, the outsourcing strategy will become yet one more non-core competency that demands considerable time and focus from management and leadership. Then, the company must find qualified providers to meet the service and cost needs of the company. Let's take a closer look at the internal baseline analysis and market research required to select a specific function or process for outsourcing.

BASELINING AND MARKET RESEARCH

One of the common mistakes a company makes once it has decided to outsource is to rush through or gloss over the baselining step in its eagerness to get started. However, this can have serious consequences and may adversely affect the future of the company because it will result in:

- Poor outsourcing selection decisions;
- Inadequate performance measurements (which will cause poor performance); and
- A rise in costs until they are higher than the current in-house function or process.

There must be a clear understanding of the economic and practical feasibility of outsourcing and the market capability to effectively provide the needed service. A company should not outsource to avoid an existing problem or rush into outsourcing because it appears to be the way to bypass poor performance. A company's impetus for outsourcing should be to accomplish positive goals — not to avoid negative circumstances. Outsourcing an ineffective function or process is not a guarantee that the function or process will work any better or cost any less than what is being done today. That is why baselining is so important — it requires a company to examine all aspects of their processes and functions before making any rash decisions.

Why Do Outsourcing Projects Fail?

According to Giga Group, only 40% of outsourcing projects undertaken are successful. Most failed outsourcing projects can be attributed to an overhasty integration of the partner into the existing environment that was not in harmony with the company's strategy. Selecting the right partner is, therefore, very important strategically and is not something that should be rushed. All too often, partnerships have been entered into as a knee-jerk reaction (for example, panic after a project or process that went wrong), and these have not been able to provide the required services in the operative environment beyond their emergency deployment. Consequently, often more harm than good comes of such partnerships, and this is neither in the interests of the customer nor the outsourcer.

The integration of an external provider in a company's proprietary business processes is an important success factor. Only a partner that can adjust itself quickly to the processes and specific needs of the customer can provide the support services required by the customer to compete successfully.[2]

A baselining and market research initiative has five basic components. They are:

- Establishing a Baseline Analysis Team;
- Defining data requirements and analysis methodology;
- Developing a baseline model;

- Performing market evaluation of service providers; and
- Developing specific outsourcing recommendations.

The sections that follow examine the steps involved in each component.

Establishing a Baseline Analysis Team

Performing a baseline analysis and performing market research are a methodical processes that should be conducted carefully and thoroughly. This is not a process that a few company leaders can undertake in one day. Therefore, the first thing a baselining and market research initiative needs is "people" to perform the tasks associated with it. Any company that has decided to outsource must establish a Baseline Analysis Team to oversee the evaluation processes. First, an executive steering team identifies the team leader and team members to complete the baseline from available internal resources.

Determining team membership is not an easy task. While the most obvious members would seem to be the staff and managers of the functions being considered for outsourcing, such team membership can be problematic. Yes, they have the knowledge necessary to provide detailed information about their functions, but they are also likely to be protective and even secretive if they think their livelihoods are at stake. Also, some people who are very capable at those processes and segments being evaluated may not be able to be objective about them. On the other hand, their knowledge is invaluable. Those creating the team should consider ways to inject objectivity; one way to do this is to consider seeking team members from an outside firm who have similar experiences in the appropriate functions. Ideally, the Baseline Analysis Team should be comprised of those with insider knowledge of your company and one or two outsiders who know the business but have nothing to protect.

The first action of the steering team should be to develop the team charter, which features the following:

- Opportunity Description/Scope — This component of the charter explains why the Baseline Analysis Team exists and what it is expected to accomplish;
- Team Process Steps — This component of the charter describes the steps the team will follow and the questions it will answer;
- Evidence of Success/Results — This critical portion of the charter describes, in measurable terms, the results the team is expected to deliver in the timeframe it has been given to meet its scope;

- Resources — This is a list of team members, team leaders, and the team liaison that also identifies those who will support the team if needed, how much time is to be spent in and out of meetings, and the additional resources available to the team;
- Constraints — This component of the charter describes the authority that the Baseline Analysis Team will have, what things the team cannot change, the team's budget, and what is outside the team's scope; and
- Expectations — This component clearly defines the team's outputs, when they are expected to be complete, and to whom they will be given.

The evidence of success/results should be quantitative measures for the team, and the expectations should include requirements for success. All members of the Baseline Analysis Team must be aligned and understand the team charter, since it will serve as a guiding document for the group. The team should hold regular business meetings and periodic checks to ensure that commitment to the charter and to the baselining initiative remains high.

The Baseline Analysis Team will communicate with the executive steering team members and their superiors to inform them of the initiative and their role in completing the work. With the steering team, they will kick off team activities with a meeting to review, revise, and approve the team charter. Then, the Baseline Analysis Team will begin the work of defining data requirements and the analysis methodology.

Defining Data Requirements and Analysis Methodology

Defining data requirements and analysis methodology is the first part of the baselining and market research initiative. You cannot collect information until you know how you're going to gather it and what you're going to do with it. This definition process starts with the development of a list of the data required to fully document *each* current function or process, including:

- Documentation of the scope of the function or process considered for outsourcing;
- Key function or process inputs through the development of process flow diagrams;
- Equipment and facilities required by the function or process;
- Staffing levels for peak and routine demand levels;

- A breakdown of the total cost of operations;
- Quality requirements;
- Measures of performance; and
- Service level and delivery requirements.

Each of these pieces is a key part of the outsourcing decision because they will all be used to determine the health, effectiveness, efficiency, quality, and cost structure of each business function.

Next, the team must identify the appropriate method for collecting data, performing the analysis, and reporting results. The goal here is to understand the current functions and to determine current requirements. You may have collected excellent and informative data, but if it is poorly presented, it will serve no real purpose. Also, if the team finds that information is missing or that it is difficult to gather certain aspects of data, there must be a plan in place to address the problems. For example, if the customer delivery requirements are not identifiable, the team may want to consider a customer satisfaction gap analysis. This type of analysis involves a series of questions directed at staff and customers to help identify discrepancies between internal requirements and customers' perceptions of satisfaction.

Considerable thought must also be given to the measures of performance or key metrics used for each process or function because these measures will become the baseline performance expected of the outsourced function. Often, effective measures of performance are not currently in place and must be developed for an outsourced function. If this is not considered up front and adequate measures are not applied to the function or process, a poor outsourcing decision may be made and it will be difficult to understand the true performance of the outsourced function.

Another tool the team can consider for the analysis portion of their task is modeling software, which is particularly useful when documenting the logistics functions or networks. The team can use it to validate the existing processes or network, summarize annual costs and customer satisfaction factors, perform a sensitivity analysis, and even model outsourcing alternatives.

Finally, the team must develop high-level selection criteria that can be applied to the analysis to make the outsourcing selection. Examples of high-level selection criteria are service levels, total cost of operations, quality and reliability of the processes, and flexibility. Once these are developed, the team should meet with the steering team and share these criteria, with the purpose of getting the steering team to agree to the criteria and support them. Next, they are ready for baseline model development. A good baseline model is critical for each business process considered a candidate for outsourcing.

Developing the Baseline Model

A baseline model is used to validate existing functional processes. The first step in developing the baseline model is to collect and analyze the following data for each outsource candidate:

- Function and process operational data — Includes data outputs for all processes involved in the function;
- Organizational structure — Addresses how the staff of each function is organized and how responsibilities flow through the function;
- Finance budgets and cost data — Includes marketing strategies and sales forecasts where applicable;
- Inventory of assets — Lists the facilities, equipment, stock, materials, supplies, and other assets, (including employees) the function has; and
- Outputs and metrics used to measure service level performance — Includes internal and external measurements and benchmarking.

The next step is to map internal business processes, which helps the team identify functional gaps, outdated methodology, and organizational issues. In this process, the team documents information flows, business rules, and so on to determine whether they meet business and mission-critical goals. Are they automated? How well are they measured? The end result of this analysis should be an issues list with the following:

- Function and process issues;
- Cost issues;
- Human resource issues;
- Technology issues;
- Regulatory issues; and
- Legal issues.

From all this information, the team will gain detailed knowledge of each business segment's processes and problems, and a map will emerge that shows each function's strengths and weaknesses.

The next step is to develop the internal cost and service level baselines. The team can take these and compare them against industry best practices to validate baselines and prepare baseline summary documents for each function or process considered a candidate for outsourcing.

These baseline summary documents will be the key to deciding what functions to outsource and what to keep in-house. Care must be taken to summarize the information correctly so it can be presented to the executive steering committee and ultimately to those making the outsourcing decisions. Therefore, the documents should be very clear and honest. This is not the time to protect interests or gloss over failures. At the same time, processes that are done well should also be given their due. After all the baseline model documents are gathered and presented, the next step is to perform a market evaluation of service providers.

Performing Market Evaluation of Service Providers

At this stage of the game, some may think it is premature to identify and evaluate service providers. After all, the company is not sure what it's going to outsource yet. Some people may believe that it is a waste of time to research providers when a function may wind up being kept in-house. However, what they may not realize is that the availability and quality of those offering services for functions being considered as outsourcing candidates impacts whether or not it is feasible to outsource a function. For example, a company may have defined its core competency as the innovative design and branding of a highly specialized product. Company leaders may feel that they should outsource the product's manufacture so that resources can be devoted to design. But, if no one out there has the capability to manufacture the product or those that have tried have done a very poor job, then perhaps outsourcing the manufacture is not a good, timely decision.

At the same time, market research adds weight to a team's outsourcing recommendation. If a team has identified a list of qualified outsourcers who can perform the function under consideration, then it makes the decision of whether or not to outsource easier, particularly if the function is either secondary core or primary non-core.

To begin the market research process, the Baseline Analysis Team should identify potential providers of the service or function. Team members may draw from their answers to the organizational chart exercise described in Chapter 4, where they listed each function and asked if they knew of another company that made the function their core competency. They may also use industry knowledge, networking, the Web, and other outside resources. This will create a list of potential providers and their capabilities that the team can evaluate as preliminary outsourcing candidates.

The next step is to prepare a request for information (RFI) to solicit a number of potential vendors for information about their products and services. This document should be detailed enough to allow a high-level due diligence of available providers. The information the respondents should provide includes:

- Company strengths and weaknesses;
- Relevant previous experience, such as a client list;
- Reference sites for similar outsourcing;
- Financial stability and growth plans;
- Availability of knowledgeable technical resources;
- Responsiveness and interest in the business; and
- Indications of company culture, such as values, employee expectations, goals, and objectives.

The team should then evaluate the RFI responses to identify potential service providers based on the following selection criteria:

- Technical ability — Do the people performing the work have up-to-date knowledge and training on the technology necessary for the job? Can they provide the level of technical services and compatibility required for the job?
- Depth of experience in the field — How long has the company been performing its services? How many clients has it had? Are site visits encouraged?
- Company and organizational culture — Does the provider have an organizational culture committed to continuous improvement? What are its goals, vision, and mission? Are its employees aligned with these? Does it have an approach and philosophy consistent with yours?
- Financial stability — What are the company's finances like? Are they a well-established company with the means to take on your company's job?

Not only will these criteria provide a greater understanding of the services offered by outsourcing providers and the market for specific services overall, but they will be useful when you are at the request for proposal (RFP) stage in your company's outsourcing initiative. Once all the evaluations have been prepared, they will become part of the process of developing specific outsourcing recommendations.

Outsourcing Vendor Selection: Boston University and IKON

Boston University used to run its own printing and copying shops on campus. In 2002, BU began evaluating ways to increase the efficiency and utilization of their existing print center. To offer better and more innovative printing and copying services, as well as cut costs, the university decided to streamline the printing and copying processes by creating one campus copy shop (Image Xpress) and outsourcing the printing. The university chose IKON to handle the printing and copying.

"We chose IKON because they came in with the best track record and the most ambitious concepts for how to improve services," says Peter Fiedler, Assistant Vice President for Boston University.

The campus-copying store handles such jobs as newsletters, flyers, and course packets. IKON has also introduced a feature whereby customers can create print-ready files on their own computers and submit them to the copy shop through the web.

Since outsourcing to IKON in 2002, the university has saved $500,000. Production volume has increased 30 percent, and, most importantly, customer satisfaction has increased and there are far fewer complaints.[3]

Developing Specific Outsourcing Recommendations

Once each business segment has its own baseline summary document and the market research is complete, it is time to make outsourcing recommendations. This is also the time when your company should revisit the goals, mission, strategic vision, and requirements discussed in Chapter 4. You should also begin understanding and determining what it will take to make sure that your primary core functions get the attention they deserve from leadership and management.

The first step in developing outsourcing recommendations is to identify those functions or processes that meet company financial return objectives. Everyone involved in the process should be able to agree whether the following statements are "True" or "False" for each function:

- This function isn't central to generating profits or competitive success.
- This function is a routine one that wastes valuable time and energy.
- This function is either temporary or it recurs in cycles.
- It's less expensive to have someone else handle this segment of business than it is to do it in-house.
- This function can be done cheaper in-house, but it drains resources that could be better used elsewhere.
- The skill(s) required for this function are so specialized that it is impractical to have regular staff do it.

Functions that earn a "False" probably should remain in-house. Those that earn a "True" are most likely good candidates for outsourcing. This exercise will lead to judicious outsourcing recommendations that will allow your company to remain competitive and succeed. You will know the potential savings, in terms of time and money, as well as potential returns on investment. You will have assessed what you can and cannot do within your company.

The next step is to prioritize the list of potential outsource providers created while the team was conducting its market research. Take a critical look at the evaluations you made based on the RFIs you received and try to determine which candidates best met the evaluation criteria. You may want to devise a scoring or rating technique of some sort, or decide which criteria carry more weight. Once the list of candidates is prioritized, you will need to obtain consensus on the prioritized list. After that, you can develop a schedule and plan for the outsourcing process as detailed in the next chapter.

---

1 Pat Lay. "Smaller Companies Spotlight," *This Is Money,* June 3, 2004. http://www.thisismoney.com/20040603/si79021.html

2 Christopher Steinhauer, "Why Make or Buy Has an Impact on the Implementation of Corporate Strategy," *Business International,* June 8, 2004. http://www.copybook.com/publications/article.asp?pubID=1&catID=566&artID=876

3 Michael F. Corbett, "Dispelling the Myths about Outsourcing," Special supplement, *Fortune,* May 31, 2004.

ON THE ELEVATOR

Most outsourcing decisions are based on the economic returns or savings compared to the cost. However, the real reason companies should outsource is the need to focus management time and resources. A clear side benefit of outsourcing is cost savings and service improvements, but the real driver needs to be management focus.

Companies must focus management time and attention on their core competencies and maintain efforts to continuously improve those functions that are core. A look at organizations' histories shows the deterioration in performance that occurs when company leaders and managers begin to focus on non-core activities. Profit performance declines and competitiveness weakens. Therefore, functions that are outside of the core should be outsourced to free management time and organizational resources to work on the highest priority activities — core competencies.

To select specific functions for outsourcing, an internal baseline analysis and market research initiative is required. This process will also help the company identify:

- Internal needs and service requirements for the functions or processes;
- The cost structure of the functions or processes that are candidates for outsourcing;
- Qualified providers that can meet the service and cost needs of the company.

Rushing the baseline development step can cause serious consequences to the future of the company, resulting in poor outsourcing selection decisions, a decline in performance, and an increase in costs.

A baselining and market research initiative has five basic components. They are:

- Establishing a Baseline Analysis Team — This team is responsible for collecting the data, analyzing it, and preparing baseline summary documents for each function;

- Defining data requirements and analysis methodology — This definition process starts with the development of a list of the data required to fully document each current function or process. Then, the team must identify the appropriate method for collecting data, performing the analysis, and reporting the results. The goal of these steps is to understand the current functions, determine current requirements, develop high-level selection criteria, and get steering team agreement;
- Developing a baseline model — The baseline model is used to validate existing functional processes. It involves collecting data about the processes, mapping the business processes, developing issues lists, developing cost and service level baselines, comparing internal baselines against industry best practices for validation, and preparing a summary document for each process considered a candidate for outsourcing;
- Performing market evaluation of service providers — This is accomplished by identifying potential providers, preparing RFIs for high-level due diligence of available providers, and evaluating the RFI responses to identify potential service providers based on selection criteria; and
- Developing specific outsourcing recommendations — In this step, the team determines the feasibility of outsourcing specific functions or processes based on the work it has done, identifies those functions or processes that meet company financial return objectives, prioritizes the list of potential outsource providers, obtains consensus on the prioritized list, and prepares for the next steps in the outsourcing process.

6 The Solicitation Process

INTRODUCTION

Once your outsourcing team has identified primary and secondary core processes and determined its outsourcing targets, it is time to solicit providers for the process or processes being outsourced. This is one of the most critical components of the outsourcing process, and it must be done properly. Surprisingly, many companies do not realize this. Many poorly developed and written RFPs have been disseminated over the years, resulting in frustrations and failed outsourcing ventures. We have seen instances where someone in a company develops a one-page scope of work, hands that over to a potential provider, and asks them to bid on a critical element of work. This is no way to establish the type of relationship necessary for successful outsourcing.

A good RFP is the foundation for a successful outsourcing venture, and therefore it should not be treated lightly. It will be sent to the top five to seven companies you select during an evaluation process and it will take time to determine who those companies will be. The general timeline for creating an RFP is nine weeks and the follow-up activities — which include releasing the RFP, evaluating responses, and final selection — can also take up to nine weeks. However, with education, buy-in, and consistent preparation, as well as a good request for information (RFI), you can develop an RFP that will lay the groundwork for an outsourcing relationship that will mature into a partnership that benefits all involved.

The steps involved in the solicitation process are:

1. Setting realistic expectations;
2. Setting goals and a timeline;
3. Developing an RFI to determine who will receive the RFP;

4. Evaluating the responses to the RFI;

5. Developing a scope of work;

6. And drafting the RFP itself.

After that, you can send the RFP out and prepare your company to evaluate the proposals you will receive. This chapter discusses the steps involved in the solicitation process, as well as the preliminary actions necessary for evaluating the proposals and bids generated by the RFP.

Setting Expectations

Surprisingly, many companies do not understand outsourcing. Therefore, the process of setting expectations for outsourcing should start with an examination of what outsourcing should accomplish and what it shouldn't. If a company is considering a 3PL, for example, it is important for those involved to understand that 3PL is the utilization of an outside firm to perform some or all of the supply chain functions an organization requires. This can involve any aspect of logistics and is more than simply outsourcing warehousing or transportation. As a rule, a 3PL service provider integrates more than one link within the overall supply chain, but the service can be as narrow or broad as needed. Therefore, the company should learn all it can about the different types of 3PLs and what they can offer. Otherwise, it will not be possible to develop an RFP with the correct elements.

Also, if you want to improve your company's supply chain, you must be aware that, in order to develop these improvements, drastic changes may have to be made within the company first to meet the improvement requirements. A client that wanted to improve their supply chain thought that hiring a 3PL would take care of that, so they did not pay attention to the processes within their company. In the end, their outsourcing initiative failed because the company's internal processes did not work with the 3PL. Your company must understand that it may need to overhaul internal processes that are not being outsourced as part of the initiative if you truly want to improve your supply chain. Similar research and education is necessary before developing an RFP for outsourcing manufacturing processes.

Therefore, some helpful questions to ask at this point are:

- Has the business case been well defined?
- What if we do nothing?
- What are the benefits of outsourcing? Does it fit into our short- and long-term business strategies?

- What are the risks?
- Have all the stake holders been identified?
- What are the required resources?

Another part of the education process needed for the development of a good RFP is to dispel myths and rumors. Often companies think if they outsource operations or operations processes, they will be relinquishing all responsibility for the process being outsourced and they fear they will lose control. This is not true. Outsourcing manufacturing, warehousing, transportation and other related processes frees your company from day to day execution, but your company remains in control of the operation. This must be stressed during the education process until everyone involved understands it. Once a clear understanding of what outsourcing is and what it will do for the company has been reached, the team can use it to achieve buy-in — on all levels, but with a particular emphasis on senior management.

Buy-in is critical at this stage, because it ensures that the RFP and selection process will move forward. It forces everyone in the company to take an inventory of emotions and allows realistic expectations to be set before any commitments are made. On several occasions, we have gotten all the way to the end of the selection process, when, suddenly, a senior manager asks a question or expresses a concern that should have been raised in the first stages of the process. For example, we were once asked

3PLs and RFPs: Dispelling the Myths

One of the things Tompkins Associates has seen in our experience with outsourcing is the false impression that 3PLs will jump on any opportunity that comes their way. In actuality, most 3PLs critically review RFPs to decide if they should pursue those opportunities. In practice, we have found that at least one third of 3PLs will drop out of the initial sourcing process. Some of the questions 3PLs ask after reviewing the RFP are:

- Does it fit our business objectives?
- Is this a customer we want?
- How much risk is there?
- Is the RFP credible and professional?
- Are they sincere about outsourcing this?
- Are we just a price check against an incumbent 3PL or perhaps against keeping it in-house?
- What differentiates us from others in the process?
- Do we have a relationship with this potential customer or are we behind before we even get started?

Therefore, a good RFP and sourcing process gets the attention of credible 3PLs and creates a competitive, best-solution contest that ultimately benefits the company outsourcing logistics.

if we should have had warehouse providers bid on an East Coast and West Coast facility rather then a central facility. Education can prevent this from happening. It also allows the team to set realistic goals and timelines, which is the next step in the RFP process.

Setting Goals and a Timeline

After everyone understands what outsourcing is and management is on board, your team can clearly set forth the goals you want the service provider to help you achieve. While you are identifying these goals, make sure you are focused on the positive. Poor performance should not be the driving force behind an outsourcing plan. As we discussed in Chapter 5, the most important goal for outsourcing is to return leadership and management focus to the levels necessary for peak performance. Examples of other positive goals include:

- Increased customer satisfaction;
- Access to world-class technology;
- Increased competitiveness;
- Cost reduction;
- Release of capital;
- Reduced future investment; and
- Reduced risk.

These goals must fit the organization's needs over the life of the relationship. At this point, you must not assume that today's level of performance is what is required for the service provider.

In the goal setting process, it is also important to involve senior management early, often, and at key decision points. You want them to understand and contribute to the goals and obtain their support. This will take some work. We recommend taking the list of goals and sharing them with everyone on the management team and anyone else from whom you need support for the outsourcing initiative to go forward. Explain why the goals are important and how you think outsourcing will help achieve them. Be sure to emphasize how each manager will benefit when the goals are achieved. Again, stress the fact that outsourcing will allow them to focus on their primary core processes as well as improve bottom-line performance.

Once the goals are in place, the team should develop a detailed, realistic timeline for the outsource process. The critical task here is to identify key dates for:

- RFI release;
- RFI response and evaluation;
- RFP release;
- RFP response;
- Site visits;
- Short list;
- Due diligence;
- Selection;
- Term sheet signing;
- Contract signing;
- Beginning implementation; and
- Completing implementation.

Once you have clearly identified your outsourcing goals and created a realistic timeline, you can develop a list of potential providers and decide which of them will receive your RFP.

Developing the List of Potential Providers

The process of developing a list of potential providers actually begins when a company's Baseline Analysis Team conducts the market research that is part of identifying your core competencies and targeting processes for outsourcing. At that time, the team researches companies that offer services that correlate with the targeted processes. Now that your company has identified the processes to be outsourced, you can take that research and use it to compile an initial list of candidates. Also, you may wish for anyone who was not involved with the baseline analysis to suggest other candidates.

If you have decided to outsource logistics, some other sources for candidates include:

- Industry magazines;
- The Leonard's Guide;
- IWLA;
- WERC;
- "The Top 10 List" publication;
- "Top 25 Logistics Companies" publication;
- Outsourced companies; and
- The Internet.

Ideally, the number of candidates on the list should be between eight and twelve and it should represent a cross-section of service providers —

regional, national, global, privately help, publicly held, established, and start-ups (new growth).

Selecting Carriers with Outside Help and Software: Unilever HPCNA

When Lever Brothers, Cheesborough Ponds, and Helene Curtis merged to create Unilever Home and Personal Care North America (HPCNA) in 1997, there was concern about suppliers being able to meet the needs of the new, larger business. When Unilever HPCNA unveiled its objective of doubling its business in five years, the transportation managers decided the three legacy truckload carrier bases would not be able to support that scale of growth.

Unilever HPCNA spends more than $200 million annually on transportation, including inbound production items, inventory positioning, stock transfers and customer shipments. The legacy truckload carrier base consisted of 80 truckload providers handling more than 200,000 shipments a year. With that many carriers and that level of spending, it was obvious there were savings opportunities at stake in addition to finding more qualified suppliers.

Unilever HPCNA decided in September 2001 to put it all out for bid at one time and realized it had to go one of two ways. "We knew if we managed the project manually we would have to select a very narrow list of carrier candidates to focus on," says Chuck Irwin, director of transportation for Unilever HPCNA.

Option two was to bring in an outside resource with the experience and software to help with the selection process. They chose a consulting group that had been working with Unilever on a strategic sourcing initiative since early 1998. With that company's guidance, Unilever HPCNA whittled the incumbent truckload supply base of 80 down to 50, eliminating 30 carriers they felt could not handle the business the larger Unilever HPCNA was bringing. From there, new truckload carriers were brought in to increase competition and lane coverage.

The company took the information and put it into its optimization software to establish the lowest-cost carriers for each lane as a baseline. From there, a variety of different constraints were layered in on top of the cost information, changing the optimal suppliers in various lanes. In about four weeks, they produced a list of target carriers for each lane that is the best carrier for each lane based on all of the factors considered. By the end of the process, Unilever HPCNA had settled on 20 carriers, ten of which were new and ten of which were incumbents, but spending and leverage with each of those carriers increased.[1]

The next step is to identify the capabilities of each company on your list. One of the best ways to accomplish this is to make an initial call and talk about timelines, your process, and initial expectations. Ask them if they know your specific industry. If you are a small company, ask them if they have provided services for small companies in the past and if they continue to do so. You probably do not want to send an RFP to a company that has only done business with Fortune 500 companies or a company that tried to work with a small customer but was not successful. If you are a big company, the opposite applies.

Your company should also not limit its list to outsource providers only; there may be industry players who can meet your requirements that are not necessarily considered outsourcers. You want to consider all viable candidates. Once you have done this, you can prepare an RFI. If you developed one as part of the process of identifying outsourcing targets, you may use it as a framework. The one you develop in this case, however, will be more specific.

Preparing the RFI

RFIs come in many shapes and sizes. There are numerous approaches and formats. The structure we find most successful includes the following:

- Introductory letter — This should state the goal of the outsource initiative and instructions for responding to the RFI;
- Intent to respond notice — This is a single page that a service provider must complete and return. It serves as a confidentiality agreement and includes the date of receipt, the company's name, contacts, the areas in the RFI that the client intends to answer; and a signature;
- Evaluation process — This should begin with a half-page, high-level outline of your company's selection process, stating key decision criteria and may include the number of finalists that will receive the RFP. After that, you go into more detail, clearly stating your timeframes, guidelines and contacts, the purpose and scope of the RFI, and your business requirements; and
- RFI questionnaire — This is often considered the true RFI exercise because it gets to the heart of the matter. The questionnaire should have two to three sections, depending on the process you are outsourcing. The two required sections are general company information and specific services information. The third section should be included if you are outsourcing technology processes. The first section should ask the respondents to provide addresses, the corporate vision and goals, the services they offer, number of employees, financial information, market share and recognized competitors, business plans, current customers, case studies, and awards and certifications. The second section should list each one of your outsourcing requirements, ask about approach and capabilities on functional specifics, request sample metrics, and inquire about the provider's competitive differences or advantages. The

third section, if applicable, should ask about the company's technology applications and their capabilities as well as service levels, including help desk and escalation processes.

When you list your outsourcing requirements in the second section of the questionnaire, it is important that you be clear and explicit. This is particularly important if your outsourcing initiative is complex or you expect more than ten responses to the RFI. For example, Tompkins Associates was engaged by a coffee company to help them find a provider for their outsourcing initiative. We made sure that our client was clear and precise when they listed their requirements, and as a result, we were able to narrow a list of 20–30 RFI respondents down to the seven that actually received the RFP.

Once you have prepared the RFI and it has the support of management, you may send it to the candidates you selected earlier. Do not be too concerned about the length of your RFI, especially the questionnaire section. In some cases, the questionnaire may have only a few questions, but it is more likely that you will have numerous questions. Remember, the more questions you ask, the easier it will be to determine if the provider is a good fit for your RFP. You will have few surprises when you receive proposals and that will mitigate risks during the selection and contracting processes.

Evaluating RFI Responses

After you have received the responses, you have several methods you can use to draw up a list of qualified respondents that should receive your RFP. One option is to use the evaluation criteria section in the RFI as a guideline. Another option is to create a scoring matrix. A third option is to create a summary of each response to your RFI that addresses the following topics:

- Capability — Does the provider have sufficient infrastructure, strengths, and capabilities to perform required services?
- Philosophy — Is the provider committed to continuous improvement?
- Financial data — Is the provider willing to report its internal costs? When combined with internal cost analysis, do they provide the data necessary for actual financial results that can be used to compare with expectations?

- Service — Are the provider's front-line people impressive? Are
  the people who might manage the operation well-versed in the
  pertinent issues? Do they encourage site visits and other communications? Has the provider submitted references that speak to requirements similar to yours and are willing to discuss the provider
  with you?
- Fit — Is the provider's approach to the process similar to yours?
- Reach — Can the provider meet global and local service requirements?
- Technology — Are the provider's information systems up to date?

The RFI summary is an excellent "weeding out process" because it
levels the respondents' playing field and it helps you zero in on key issues
and qualities. It is also an excellent tool for directing senior management
focus on only qualified providers because it provides a granular level of
information quickly.

Any of the three options will help you evaluate the RFIs; which one
you choose depends on your process and your company's culture. You
can be creative when necessary. For example, Tompkins Associates helped
a large industrial manufacturer find a group of providers to receive their
RFP for outsourcing very labor-intensive processes that involved kitting,
product overlap, and value-added services that were difficult to describe
on paper. We invited the potential vendors to fly in and view the processes
first-hand to make sure they could handle them and, based on their reactions, we were able to determine who would receive the RFP.

Once you have applied your evaluation methodology, you will have
a solid list of companies to receive the RFP. Your next step is to draft
the RFP that you will send them. The first thing you will need is a
scope-of-work.

Scope-of-Work

An RFP is what you use to communicate your expectations to potential
service providers. However, before you draft the RFP, your company
must first identify these expectations. You do that by developing a
scope-of-work, which should have the following:

- A general description of the processes involved;
- Operational data and current process maps (base data with growth
  potential and a detailed description of current or desired processes
  — if the processes do not currently exist — so that potential

providers can understand the magnitude of the volume and the amount of effort required to do the work);

- Detailed reporting requirements;
- What tasks are to be performed;
- Expected growth and change in business in the future;
- The level of performance desired; and
- A list of all the external factors that affect the process.

You should also include the current benchmark costs of performing the work, and any fee structure options you want to be considered. You must clearly state hours and days of operations, and include any special services that do not fall under the normal schedule. Once the scope is defined, the team should make sure that the boundaries of what is to be outsourced are clearly established.

The scope-of-work must include input from the people currently involved in the process that will be outsourced and any other processes within the company that the outsourced process touches. We also recommend that your company consult with an outside resource that is experienced in outsourcing that process. Gathering input from internal and external resources is important because:

- The people performing the job at present know what is involved in the process;
- Varying points of view can better help you gauge qualitative advantages/disadvantages of the current process;
- Those performing the work that will be outsourced have the greatest potential to sabotage the outsourcing process and involvement may deter them;
- Input from external and internal resources will help you develop more accurate cost estimates and lower the incidence of start-up problems; and
- An outside resource will be able to provide unbiased evaluation of bids and assistance in the selection process.

Combining these different points of view is the best way to deal with the problem of vested interest vs. objectivity as you create the scope-of-work. Having an external resource involved in this process removes emotional ties and bias, adds professionalism, and keeps participants focused on execution. Without this objectivity, there is the danger of duplicating existing poor processes in the scope-of-work and reinventing the wheel.

Drafting the RFP

Once you have developed the scope-of-work, you have the framework for an RFP. This document not only spells out your requirements for service (including the scope-of-work), but it gives prospective service providers the information they need to prepare a bid.

As we mentioned earlier in this chapter, companies often approach drafting the RFP with less care than writing an email. This only hurts the company because a poorly written RFP can result in frustration, wasted time and money, and, ultimately, failure. An RFP is the template for a provider's contract with a company, and if the provider does not know what the company contracting with them expects, a long contract negotiation is a certainty. Both parties might end up pushing away from the table and deciding that it's not worth the effort to do business together.

Therefore, an RFP should provide potential providers with a clear set of requirements, a clear path forward, and a clear desire for innovation and creativity. It does not tell candidates how to do their job; instead, it informs them of what needs to be done. It sets forth a company's full range of volume requirements to include slow, typical and high levels of activity.

A good RFP has the following structure:

- Introduction — This is a high-level section that identifies the services to be outsourced, states objectives; provides an overview of what is in the RFP; defines what is out of scope; and touches on bid options and different scenarios;
- Scope-of-work — This is the scope-of-work discussed in the previous section. It should also include a history of your company and your business requirements;
- Instructions to bidder — This part of the RFP tells bidders your company's intentions, the timetables involved, and how to submit bids, including how many copies of their proposal you wish to receive and a copy of a proposal pricing form. It should describe correspondence control, how you plan to receive and answer questions from the bidders, and what you require in the way of responses, including format;
- Company information — In this section, you request that bidders provide evidence that they can meet your requirements, including a statement of their capabilities, financial statements, client references, project descriptions or case studies, and resumes of those who comprise their management and proposed project implementation teams;

- Account management — This section describes how you will manage their account and sets forth your reporting requirements, how the account will be serviced (including an escalation path for problems), strategic relationships, the project schedule, and access to any online communications and documentation libraries;
- Performance expected during due diligence and site visits — Providers must know that they will be asked to show an existing process in their company that is close to the process being out-sourced;
- Terms and conditions — These are standard terms and conditions that serve as a template for a future contract;
- Evaluation criteria — This section is where you inform bidders of those factors that will drive your choice of provider including cost, their ability to meet established metrics, their experience, their strengths, and the accuracy and completeness of their response to the RFP; and
- Documentation to be included — This can include more detailed resumes, annual reports, financial statements, and any other information you request (such as AutoCAD® layouts or evidence of design work or system design if applicable).

The most important thing to remember when you draft an RFP is that it must be comprehensive, clear, and honest. Share as much information as you can. That is the only way you will receive clear, comprehensive, and honest proposals in return. An outsourcing venture is doomed from the outset if the customer and vendor are still discovering information about each other during the term of the contract. This will happen if you are not up-front in the very beginning.

Once your outsourcing team has drafted the RFP, the next move is simple: send the RFP to the list of potential providers you identified when you evaluated the responses to the RFIs. The next step in the process, evaluating the RFP responses, is discussed in the next chapter.

---

1 David Hannon. "Unilever Leans on Software to Optimize Spend." *Purchasing*, 11 Dec. 2002. http://www.manufacturing.net/article/CA264898?search=web-exclusive&text=rfp

ON THE ELEVATOR

Once your outsourcing team has identified primary and secondary core processes and determined its outsourcing targets, it is time to solicit providers for the processes being outsourced. This is one of the most critical components of the outsourcing process, and it must be done properly. To prepare an RFP that will allow you to select the best provider, you must take the following actions:

- Clearly set forth the goals to be achieved by outsourcing, keeping in mind that your primary goal will be to return leadership and management focus to the levels necessary for peak performance. Do not assume that today's level of performance is what is required for the service provider. The goals must fit the organization's needs over the life of the relationship.
- Develop a detailed, realistic timeline for the outsource process. Identify key dates such as RFP release, RFP response, site visits, short list, due diligence, selection, term sheet signing, contract signing, beginning implementation, and completing implementation.
- Involve senior management early, often, and at key decision points. Be certain senior management understands the scope, goals and timeline. Set realistic expectations. Obtain leadership support.

- Be certain that a wide range of candidates are pre-qualified before sending the RFP. Consider outsource providers as well as industry players. Perform extensive research to be certain all viable candidates are asked to bid by creating an RFI that clearly defines your needs and evaluating the responses to those needs;
- Clearly define the scope of what is to be outsourced. Once the scope is defined be sure that the boundaries of what is to be outsourced are clearly established.
- Establish benchmarks for the cost of self-performing and expected service levels that will serve as a baseline for the outsourced activity.
- Be certain the RFP provides a clear set of requirements, a clear path forward, and a clear desire for innovation and creativity. Use the RFP to tell people what needs to be done. Do not use the RFP to tell potential providers how to do their jobs. Be certain the full range of volume requirements is set forth to include slow, typical, and high levels of activity.
- Share the outsourcing process and timeline with each qualified provider. Be sure all candidates are given the same information and opportunity to present their best bid.

Request for Proposal and Service Provider Selection

INTRODUCTION

Choosing the best service provider is an obvious key to success in an outsourcing initiative. Because of the impact outsourcing has on a company's bottom line, failure is not an option. Therefore, you must have a methodical bid evaluation and provider selection process, one that should not be rushed even when there are time constraints or there is pressure to make a decision quickly. The selection process can be time consuming and costly, but the good news is that there are time-tested and true methodologies that can help you make the right decision.

The process begins with the creation of a selection team, followed by short-listing, and then final selection. Once the selection is made, the legal relationship begins; however, you must involve your legal team in the selection process, especially after you have determined your short list. This will be discussed in more detail in chapter nine.

Another important factor in the process is cultural fit, which is often not considered part of the evaluation criteria. This is a mistake because it has been proven that when the cultures of two companies clash the outsourcing process becomes an uphill battle that typically starts on Day One and ends in termination or even litigation. This chapter discusses creating the selection team, the short list, the final evaluation, cultural fit, and the post-selection process.

SELECTION TEAM

A team approach is critical to the RFP evaluation and final selection; in fact, it is really the only approach. The makeup of this team is also critical and should include members from all functional areas that touch the function being outsourced. The representatives should have a good understanding of the process being outsourced and, ultimately, should be involved with the outsource provider in some capacity. For example, you should think about including members from the following areas:

- Operations – Warehousing, Transportation, Manufacturing;
- Finance;
- Technology;
- Legal;
- Human Resources;
- Customer Service; and
- Sales.

Often, a poor outsourcing provider selection is the result of not including enough company representatives on the selection team. For example, many companies fail to include someone from the legal department because they believe that lawyers are only necessary for drafting and negotiating the contracts. This is a mistake. You should involve legal early in the process of selection. This is discussed in more detail in chapter nine.

Also, having the wrong people involved in the selection can easily result in making the wrong decision. For example, if you have a number of people from the same department or a number of members with the same perspectives, you run the risk of reaching a consensus too quickly and possibly making a subjective rather than objective decision. Therefore, your team should include no more than one to two representatives from each functional area.

Also, while including representatives from the process being outsourced is key, you must stay aware of the fact that they are most likely resistant to the idea of outsourcing their functions. Their personal bias may affect the decision process adversely and their input should be carefully considered. One of the best methods is using representatives from the functions that will be interfacing with the provider. They will ultimately have the relationship with the provider. This can also prevent the finger-pointing after implementation because they were part of the selection committee and have a stake in the success of the relationship.

Ultimately, there should be one point person that is out in front and is responsible for the relationship as a whole. This individual must be capable of seeing both sides of a situation and be constantly striving for a win/win solution. People who go at this with a win/lose mentality will ultimately hurt the overall relationship and possibly contribute to the failure of the outsourcing engagement as a whole.

Once you have chosen your representatives, you should pick one to be the single point of contact between the team and the companies whose proposals are being evaluated. This contact will handle all information, questions, and answers between the team and the potential providers. This is the most effective way to control communications during the evaluation process because it ensures that the companies will receive consistent communications that have been agreed upon by the team.

The timeframe for evaluation and the proposed implementation date generally determine the frequency of the team meetings. In the meetings, there are definite issues that need to be determined. These include:

1. Overall schedule;
2. Due diligence visit dates (should be attended by team);
3. Development of evaluation criteria, weights and understanding of consistent application; and
4. Final evaluation meeting and recommendation of service provider.

Once you have made the decisions necessary for creating a strong selection team, the team can begin the selection process. To make the selection process more manageable, the team should break it down into two steps. The first step is to reduce the RFP respondents down to a short list, which, ideally, is comprised of three go-forward candidates. Then, you should apply a more rigorous assessment to the short list based on final evaluation criteria.

THE SHORT LIST

Creating the short list requires some effort and may involve reading the proposals several times. The first step is to check all the proposals to see if they address the full scope of the functions to be outsourced and to make sure that there are names and numbers for credit references and clients. Those potential providers who sent incomplete proposals can then be eliminated before serious work begins.

The next step is to review the proposals to search for viable candidates. You may wish to draw up a list of questions about the proposals, such as:

- Does the proposal demonstrate familiarity with your industry? Or does it use a lot of buzzwords to imply knowledge that the company really does not have?

- Does the proposal demonstrate the company's financial stability? Or are financials glossed over in an attempt to disguise problems?
- Does the proposal demonstrate that the company provides the appropriate services necessary for your outsourcing initiatives? Or does it try to sell other services because it is better qualified to handle those?
- Does the proposal demonstrate that the provider is organized in its approach to a project? Or is the company "all over the map" in its description of processes?
- Are the proposal's terms and conditions clear, fair, and appropriate? Or will it take the efforts of a legal team similar to that representing a defendant in a corporate accounting scandal to unravel them?

While it is very important for you to examine and understand the proposals, you need not rely solely on them to determine who meets the criteria necessary for short-listing. There are other actions you can take that complement and supplement the proposal review. These activities include:

- Checking references — You should call the respondents' customers to gain insights into each candidate's performance. A good way to do this is to use the same evaluation criteria used to create an RFI summary and ask the customers to comment on each. You might also ask each reference to give examples of how the provider recovered from a difficult situation, such as poor service levels.
- Face to face meetings — Invite respondents to visit your company and make oral presentations. It is important to keep in mind, however, that the oral presentations must be considered supplemental to the proposal. Providers will send a sales team to try and impress you with glossy and glitzy presentations, but in the end, it is the provider and not their sales team that will be doing the work, and you must remember that.
- Operations site visits — Touring each candidate's facilities, usually more than one, can help you determine if they are viable providers whose culture fits with yours (discussed in more detail in a later section), especially if you feel you've been dazzled by a powerful sales presentation during the face to face meetings. You can see how the provider works and ask questions of the people involved in their operations. For the initial site visits, it is best if only two

or three members of your selection team visit. Later visits should include more team members.

- Post-proposal communications review — Examine each candidate's responses to your questions and other communications about their proposals. In large firms, proposals are often subjected to a thorough internal editorial review before they are sent out. Many times those doing the work may contribute some information to it, but professional communicators package it. It is important to see how candidates think "on the fly" and to determine how well the actual people doing the work will interact with your company should they be selected.

Throughout the proposal review and the activities surrounding it, the members of the selection team should be comparing companies to one another and taking detailed notes, not just on the companies but on the members' own responses to the proposals. Ask specific, clear questions of yourselves and the respondents. Be sure that those members of the team who paid visits to potential provider sites have documented their experiences completely. It might take some time, many meetings, and perhaps a few headaches, but in the end, you will have arrived at a short list of contenders and then the rigorous evaluation of the finalists to determine which will get the project can begin.

FINAL EVALUATION

Contrary to popular belief, deciding which of the providers on your short list will be your outsourcer involves more than contacting the provider with the lowest bid and beginning the contract negotiation process. Yes, cost is an important factor in your decision and it is a key differentiator if you have two equally qualified candidates, but it must not be the only one. Instead, you must develop a list of weighted criteria (one that includes cost) and rank each element.

There are many different evaluation criteria you can use in your final evaluation. Which ones you use, and their relative weightings, depends on the end objectives of the project and what is important to your company. For example, if you are outsourcing manufacturing/assembly, your criteria and their weights might differ from that of logistics, warehousing, and distribution. The size of your project will also determine the weight assigned to your criteria. There are, however, certain criteria that should

Why does it always come down to cost?

Although it should not be the driving factor, without fail, cost becomes the final factor in the outsourcing selection process. Many say this is the way it should be, but basing the selection of a provider solely on the fact that their bid was the lowest can have serious repercussions that might even drive up the costs of your outsourcing initiative.

Here are some things to consider while you are considering costs during the evaluation process:

- Can the provider really provide the services you need at the price quoted? Low bids often result in poor service levels—do you really want that?
- To keep in line with the price quoted in the company's proposal, will the provider take measures to economize that are a negative reflection on your company? For example, will it use an older building with poorly maintained machinery, old trucks, or out-of-date manufacturing environments?
- Will the relationship last over the long-term? The cost of sourcing a new provider if the initial relationship fails because of draconian cost-cutting measures will likely eliminate any perceived savings.
- Will the low bid result in a product and services at a standard lower than your company's? Yes, the provider may be able to pick and pack the product, but it is of no use to you if the process is haphazard and the boxes are old and worn.

So cost is certainly a factor, but as you can see, it is only one of many. In a well-managed outsourcing relationship, costs can be driven out with the following:

- Continuous Improvement programs;
- Gain sharing programs;
- Realistic budgets;
- Clear expectations;
- Constant communications, and;
- Cost-plus pricing scenarios.

We strongly recommend that you do not make cost the final factor. To do so sets the provider up for failure before they even begin. For example, Tompkins was recently involved in a major 3PL selection with multiple potential vendors. Over a period of several weeks, a list of viable contenders was created based on provider capability and a fit with the client's business. At that point, cost became the driver, and our client set a realistic and industry goal.

To leverage cost, the client kept driving down the price to hit the competitive market goal. As a result, several of the providers drove their prices down below the market goal, while others were eliminated. At this point, we determined the project was in jeopardy because it was not likely that the work could be done at the costs quoted by the finalists. In the end, the client chose the provider with the highest price. So, was that the best value for the money? Only time will tell. It is possible that by initiating the bidding war, the client eliminated a better provider.

be included and weighted in your final evaluation, no matter what your project. Some examples of the criteria are:

- Financial stability — Does the candidate have excellent credit and bank references? Does it have a solid financial statement?
- Service offerings — Does the candidate provide the services detailed in the functional requirements portion of the RFP?
- Culture — Does the candidate share your philosophy and values? Are its mission and strategic goals in line with yours?
- Customer Satisfaction — What have customers said about their relationships with the candidate? Will the candidate seek and use input from your customers to improve the level of service? Will the candidate be able to maintain and exceed current levels of service?
- Operations — Does the candidate use the appropriate methods, resources, and processes to assure operational efficiency and effectiveness? Does it have procedures in place that protect against equipment breakdown and malfunction? How does the candidate assure continuous improvement? If the outsourcing process requires using the candidate's facilities, what is the availability and location of essential and critical resources (for example, usable warehouse space, dock capacity, security, qualified labor, and so forth)?
- Technology — Does the candidate use technology effectively to operate its business? Does it have access to the world class technology you would use if you were keeping the process in-house? Is the candidate committed to investing in new technologies that can improve processes?
- Cost — Does the candidate's bid cover all requested items with the necessary degree of detail? Will the candidate make an acceptable profit? How does the bid compare with others of equal capability?
- Flexibility — Does the potential provider operate its company so that it can change with your needs and the needs of your customers? Is the candidate willing to make adjustments? If you have to make significant changes, will the candidate be able to respond?
- Systems — Do the candidate's information systems enable the sharing of a wide variety of information securely? Does the candidate possess or can it develop, install, and operate the same or better information systems than you currently use? What will it take to integrate its systems with yours?

Once you have identified your criteria, you apply it to each candidate. It is often helpful to create a matrix or scoreboard to use in your final evaluation. All selection team members must rate the short-listed proposals against the criteria. Performance categories should be listed and rated on a scale of one to five, with five being the best rating.

An example of an assessment method that can help you with the final evaluation is shown in the table below. It features suggested performance categories and weightings.

Category	Category Rating	Weight	Category Score	Maximum Score
Financial Stability	5	15	75	75
Service Offerings	4	15	60	75
Culture	4	15	60	75
Customer Satisfaction	3	15	45	75
Operations	3	10	30	50
Technology	4	10	40	50
Cost	2	10	20	50
Flexibility	3	5	15	25
Control Systems	5	5	25	25
Total			370 (74%)	500

Table 1: Suggested Performance Categories and Weightings

Weighting can vary from project to project depending on the goals of the outsourcing initiative. In most cases, price is at or near the top, but we have been involved with some where price was second to customer satisfaction and brand recognition. Each engagement will vary, and that is why it is important that team members represent touch points for the provider within the company. Each category should be weighted to reflect its relative importance. The total of all weights is 100, which yields a maximum score of 500 points.

Ratings are based on qualitative and quantitative assessments. The category rating is multiplied by the category weight to obtain a category score. The total of the category scores is then divided by the maximum score to obtain a performance index. The highest performance index indicates the best candidate and, by default, the provider you have selected for your outsourcing initiative.

This type of activity may appear complex and difficult, but it is vital to the evaluation and selection process because it provides the clearest picture of each candidate's capabilities. Without that picture, there is the possibility that you will make a selection that could be devastating to your organization. Using this assessment method is the best way to assure that there is a good fit between you and your provider, one that most likely will lead to a harmonious, beneficial relationship.

CULTURAL FIT

In the evaluation process, how the potential provider's company culture stands up against yours is important because, ultimately, outsourcing is about people. We have learned that, more often than not, outsourcing initiatives with high success rates involve two companies whose cultures mesh. When there is a solid cultural fit between an outsourcer and a service provider, communication flows and challenges are met and overcome.

We recently worked with a client who went through a very strenuous selection process for outsourcing their distribution processes. Because of a bad experience, the client had a perception that large global distribution providers would prove to be cold and uninterested in their business. However, we encouraged them to use a global provider, and, in the end, the client was absolutely surprised by the global provider. Their people were knowledgeable and professional, winning "hands down" on culture. What the client experienced was the value of a global provider with a strong regional feel.

Then, several months later, we had the opportunity to represent another client with similar outsource requirements but in another geographic region. As a result of the success with the previous client, we invited the same provider to bid on the RFP. The result was a disappointment. Although it was the same company, with the same process, and the same pitch, the differences between the client's approach and the provider's approach were too great. This was a well-learned lesson not soon forgotten.

At the same time, cultural fit can be difficult to measure and certainly subjective. Some examples of things to consider regarding a provider's culture while you are evaluating their bid include:

- Do they share your values? In other words, do they approach quality, cost position, human resources, and the community the same way your company does?
- Are they open with you when they answer your questions?
- Is working with them easy for you?

- Are their interactions natural rather than forced?
- Do they genuinely appear to want the opportunity? In other words, are they excited and enthusiastic about the possibility of working with your company?

While you determine the answers to these questions, you must keep in mind the fact that often a potential provider's "front men" share your cultural values but the entire organization does not. To determine whether the organization shares them at all levels, you should incorporate company culture investigation into your site visit(s). In other words, make sure, when you are touring a potential provider's facilities or observing their processes, that you have access to the people doing the actual work.

Take some time and ask the workers questions and gauge their reactions. Are they enthusiastic and helpful? Do they seem to enjoy what they're doing? Do they demonstrate substantial knowledge of the processes or facility you are observing? Are they experts or do they demonstrate a high degree of experience?

By combining your experiences in face-to-face meetings with company leaders and talking to workers on the floor during site visits, you will have multiple data points for determining whether the company's culture fits with yours. If the workers project ideas and attitudes similar to those of their leaders and sales team and they are in line with yours, most likely you will have a solid contender for your final selection.

Cultural Fit: IKON and UPS Logistics Group

After deciding to outsource its service parts distribution, IKON Office Solutions, Inc., issued a Request for Proposal to ten third-party providers and then whittled that down to a short list of five candidates. Three semi-finalists were identified after the 3PLs made presentations to IKON. After the semi-finalists were selected, members of IKON's team visited the companies. These site visits gave IKON the opportunity to get a gut feel for each provider's management culture. "If the cultures don't match, the partnership is not going to work," said an IKON representative.

  IKON did not simply meet with executives and management. To delve deeply into each candidate's company culture, IKON started at each 3PL site's receiving operation and worked their way through the facility. For example, one representative spent a half hour at an inventory control desk with warehouse workers, not only to observe what they were doing but also to see how they responded to questions, how enthusiastic they were, and whether they had the right tools.

  After comparing cultures of the semi-finalists to their own, IKON ultimately selected UPS Logistics Group to manage parts and supplies distribution.[1]

POST SELECTION

It is important to remember that a potential provider responding to a medium to large outsourcing initiative can spend upwards of $75,000 during the bid process. Therefore, after you have made your selection, you must remember to thank the participants that did not make the short list and notify them that finalists have been chosen. In the excitement of having chosen a provider and the flurry that surrounds the beginning of the new relationship and the contract negotiations, this courtesy is often forgotten.

When you thank the respondents, we recommend that you share with each why they were not the best match this time out. It is very frustrating for a provider to learn that it has not been selected for a project without being told who was or why a different selection is made. Being open and honest with them, but with tact and diplomacy, can ease frustrations and your input may even help them as they prepare to respond to other RFPs. Ending the selection process on a good note will also benefit your company because you never know when you might run across the provider again or even require their services at some point in the future.

At the same time, you should not tell any potential provider they are "the winner" until after a binding term sheet or contract is signed. Until a binding relationship is established, you should always retain more than one option. In fact, for large outsourcing initiatives, it is appropriate to hold detailed, binding term sheet discussions with more than one potential provider. This will be discussed in the chapters that follow.

---

1 Leslie Hansen Harps. "Service Parts Logistics: Taking it Outside." *Inbound Logistics,* February 2002. http://www.inboundlogistics.com/articles/features/0202_feature02.shtml

ON THE ELEVATOR

Evaluating proposals and choosing your final candidate is a time consuming process. A key thing to keep telling yourself is "Success is all in the details." You must stay focused and consider all angles when you evaluate proposals.

Here are some tips for a successful evaluation:

- Deciding who will do the evaluation is as important as how to do it. The team that will do the evaluation should come from a variety of different "touch points" with the outsourced function. This cross functional team should have a good understanding of the function being outsourced and should ultimately be involved with the outsource provider in some capacity. A word of caution: having the wrong people involved in the selection can easily result in making the wrong decision. Be sure to exclude people with an up-front bias.

- It is important to control communications with all potential providers while the evaluation process is ongoing. A single point of contact should be communicating with the potential providers. All providers should be given the same information and all questions and answers to the providers should be handled through the contact.

- The evaluation process is a business decision, not a low-cost or a personal preference. The process must be methodical. Relationships and executive preferences should not be overly emphasized. The evaluation criteria must be rigorously applied in a fair and equitable manner.

- The evaluation process should not be rushed. Often, time pressures are present, but these pressures should not result in

the team allowing the process to be anything other than fair, detailed, and robust.

- Have a clear understanding of how your team will be handling short list determination, second visits, and additional information requests. Be sure the short list process is followed and the evaluation team and process are maintained through the short list and ultimate selection process.

- Be sure to evaluate proposals and not sales presentations. The written bid is what should be evaluated. In a similar way, you must evaluate the potential provider's company as a whole and not its sales team.

- Bids are often complex. Be sure all bids address the full scope of the functions to be outsourced. Be sure the evaluation is "apples to apples" and "oranges to oranges." Examine the details of the pricing and do the arithmetic on the pricing proposal for benchmark levels. Do not make assumptions or take the bids at face value.

- Contact at least three customers of each potential provider and obtain insights into the provider's performance. Ask a standard set of questions and be certain to obtain provider feedback on everything that gives you concern. If appropriate, go visit customers and view their performance first-hand.

- Until a binding relationship is established, you should always retain more than one provider option. Therefore, do not tell any potential provider they are "the winner" until after a binding term sheet or contract is signed. For larger outsourced contracts, it is appropriate to hold detailed, binding term sheet discussions with more than one potential provider.

Creating the Outsourcing Relationship

INTRODUCTION

Once you have selected the best provider for your outsourcing initiative, you will be eager to move forward. You have plans, deadlines, and product and your company is ready to focus on its primary core functions. You must be careful at this point. Successes and failures in outsourcing initiatives are often attributable to the relationships developed between the client and outsourcing provider, rather than to business issues. After a company selects an outsourcing provider, there is a tendency to devote a lot of time to defining the outsourcing process, what metrics will be used, IT coordination, and more. The company and the provider spend much less time communicating or understanding that the relationship between a client and an outsourcer is a partnership. This is a mistake.

Outsourcing requires giving up internal control of a business function and trusting others to handle this function for you. Many have an intellectual understanding of this fact, but, emotionally, they have a hard time accepting it. Rather than just a business tool, outsourcing is a new way to think about business and requires a different thought process. Therefore, the relationship between a supplier and a customer is not the same as the relationship between a company and a provider. It is very important that everyone associated with outsourcing clearly understand these differences.

The relationship between you and your outsourcing provider cannot be taken lightly. It is not a "hands-off" process. In fact, this relationship is critical to the success of your initiative. Creating, establishing, and managing it is not easy. Much of the great relationship built during the selection process is lost or misconstrued in the actual long-term operation and what remains will form, adjust, and re-form over time. Often companies fail to build relationships with their providers that allow for these fluctuations. However, with hard work, determination, and constant open and honest communication, you can have a flexible relationship that will mutually benefit all parties involved.

The first step in this process is creating the outsourcing relationship, which involves:

- Getting the relationship started.
- Determining the relationship structure.
- Selecting a fee structure.
- Validation (relationship due diligence).
- Setting realistic timeline expectations.

This chapter focuses on creating the relationship and examines the activities above. The main goal is to effectively evolve what was understood or perceived in the selection process into a working relationship that takes you through the contracting process to implementation. Throughout this process, you must communicate openly, honestly, and without bias. Otherwise, you will be left with false perceptions, unrealistic goals, lowered expectations, and a weak relationship that may jeopardize your entire outsourcing initiative. Establishing and managing the relationship are covered in later chapters.

GETTING THE RELATIONSHIP STARTED

By its nature, outsourcing brings together at least two organizations with individual internal structures, terminology, information capabilities, and operating philosophies. As a result, many outsourcing relationships start poorly, and a poor start leads to an ineffective relationship. A failed relationship can lead to complicated and costly legal battles.

Therefore, as soon as is practicable, you should create a new team — the implementation team — comprised of members of both companies to begin the process of creating your relationship. The purpose of the team is to establish multiple touch points between your company and your provider and should go beyond the provider's sales organization and your outsourcing team and involve the people who are actually going to do the work. Therefore, the members of the team should come from two different groups of people — those who understand implementation and project management and those who will be responsible for the day-to-day business of the partnership. All team members should be current on the RFP, the solution and the negotiation on the term sheet and contract.

Once you have created the implementation team, its first task is to get the relationship started. This involves the following actions:

- Set initial expectations.
- Identify resources up-front.
- Determine where you are now and your destination.
- Develop a plan for resistance.

The sections that follow explore these aspects of getting the outsource relationship started.

Set Initial Expectations

Client-outsourcing provider relationships are labeled as failures when one party does not do what they other party expects. Most often, this is a result of mistakes providers and clients make early in the process. For example, providers commonly oversell themselves, set expectations that are too high, fail to gain a true understanding of why the client is outsourcing, and involve themselves with a member of the client's organization that is not the decision maker. The mistakes clients might make include holding back information, putting someone who is opposed to outsourcing in charge of the initiative, assuming that an outsider can fill in the company's internal information gaps, and providing an inadequate picture of operations. Trying to repair these mistakes and the damage they can cause can be very difficult. It is better to invest your energy into preventing them than fixing them. Setting expectations early is the best measure for avoiding these mistakes.

Setting expectations begins on the day of the first sales call and should continue through implementation, integration, and operations. This process requires full disclosure, open communications, and accurate information among all parties. For example, a client that provides little useful information regarding its logistics processes forces a 3PL to base its operations on assumptions and extrapolations rather than on real data. As implementation goes live both parties may be in for a number of surprises. Most often, volumes are not as high as the 3PL expected, resulting in costs that are too high and negotiated rates that are too low for the operation to be profitable.

As with any relationship, honesty is the best policy when you discuss expectations. Do not attempt to hide strategic plans or cloak the project in an air of secrecy by labeling some discussions as confidential or "off-line." If you are honest with your provider, they are more likely to be honest with you. By treating them as a partner, making them privy to your goals and plans, they will be encouraged to treat you the same way, and together you can work together to set realistic service expectations candidly and openly.

Jointly Identify Resources Up-front

In today's competitive environment, outsourcing providers can be influenced by the need not only to keep proposed costs within your budget, but also to make sure they have the lowest price. At the same time, they may promise services they may not be able to deliver at rates they have persuaded you (and themselves) are achievable. In many cases, the provider might not know the real cost of providing the services until well into the implementation process. This is compounded when you do not know your own costs of providing the service. Therefore, as part of getting your outsourcing relationship started, you and your provider should work together to identify the resources needed to perform the outsourcing functions.

It is important to remember that resources need to be identified in all areas impacting the relationship's success, including financial resources, operations, legal and technical resources. It is also vitally important to clearly identify the roles and responsibilities of the resources involved in the relationship. It is important that all parties have a clear understanding of who will be doing which tasks; therefore, you and your provider should explore all boundaries for responsibilities. The responsibilities must be communicated to both organizations to ensure everyone is aligned.

As many of the roles of individuals change during an outsource engagement it is also important to choose people with the correct background to execute these responsibilities. For example, the logical choice for handling a 3PL contract might be a warehouse manager, but you must also keep in mind the fact that an excellent warehouse manager may be an expert in that field, but not an expert on outsourcing a warehousing operation. In other words, the process of outsourcing an operation is not the same as performing the operation you are intending to outsource. This might be the time to decide that outsourcing some responsibilities may require outside assistance.

Once you have jointly identified resources and roles and responsibilities, you are ready to work with the team to discuss the goals you want the outsourcing provider to help you achieve.

Determine Where You Are Now and Your Destination

During the process of identifying core and your outsourcing targets, you collected a great deal of data that helped you establish your company's current baseline and allowed you to determine the goals you planned to achieve by using an outsourcing provider. After you have set initial expectations and identified resources with one another, now is the time to share this information with the provider.

Basically, you need to take the time to tell them where you are and then discuss where you want the outsourcing initiative to take both of you. In other words, you and your selected provider need to set outsourcing goals and determine how to achieve and measure success. To do this, we recommend using a process similar to the goal-setting exercise discussed in Chapter 4 but tailor your questions to the outsourcing initiative as follows:

- Where do we want this outsourcing initiative to take us?
- How will we get there?
- What is the science of the initiative?
- What values will we practice?
- How will we measure success?

After the team has discussed the goals and everyone is clearly on the same page, you can work together to determine how you can successfully achieve them. A major area where surprises can destroy relationships is lack of agreement on what is meant by success. It is critical that time is spent early on to define and determine performance measures. The requirements for success you defined while identifying core and non-core processes can serve as the basis for this process. Look at each requirement and think how it can be applied to the outsourcing initiative. From there, the team can devise a set of criteria for measuring the initiative's success.

Plan for Resistance

Typically, when a company announces that it is planning an outsourcing initiative, the reaction internally is to oppose the project. This backlash is unfortunately inevitable and, therefore, you must have plans for easing staff concerns, which include the following:

- Fear of the unknown (outsourcing means change and most people fear change because they don't know what it will bring);
- Fear that they will lose their jobs (many employees believe that outsourcing is synonymous with downsizing);

- Fear that outsourcing will mean additional work (some employees will wonder if a loss of jobs will mean that those who do not lose their jobs will have to do more);
- A lack of understanding of what outsourcing means (many people buy into the perception that outsourcing means offshoring);
- Fear that they will become the provider's employees and have to adjust to new and different cultures;
- Perception of a loss of power (some employees will feel helpless and powerless); and
- Uncertainty about how to deal with a new entity.

To help ease the above concerns, you should do the following:

- Communicate openly, honestly, and frequently — conduct meetings that explain why you are outsourcing and accent the positive aspects of the initiative while taking care to address the changes it will bring. If you feel employees have something to contribute, ask for feedback (however, you should keep control of this process to make sure it does not deteriorate into a round of angry accusations);
- Share your roll out plans — explain the initiative's timetable and what implementation will mean;
- Emphasize the close relationship and partnering aspect of outsourcing;
- Have the provider conduct face to face communication with your staff — this allows the employees to put "a face" to the situation whereby the provider is transformed from a faceless threatening entity into a real person;
- Provide placement services for those individuals who will not be part of the future or do not wish to be;

It is important to remember that addressing internal staff concerns is not a one-shot deal. Resistance is inevitable and you will face it throughout the initiative. Therefore, you might have to take the steps outlined above a number of times. Do not be discouraged — eventually, most resistance will recede. Meanwhile you can use the process of easing concerns to strengthen your relationship with the provider as you strive to structure your relationship.

DETERMINING THE RELATIONSHIP STRUCTURE

Each provider-client relationship is unique with no absolutes. Fundamentally, the structure of the relationship between the outsourcer and provider is based on how each reacts to the other day to day. However, you must not use this uniqueness as an excuse for not defining the type of relationship you want to have with your provider. You and the selected outsourcing provider must take the time to determine the basis of your relationship, identify how all parties will interact, and determine the structure of your relationship.

Structure is important. You are more likely to have a successful relationship with your provider if you both focus on the structure of the relationship. In fact, the Outsourcing Research Council found that 3PL relationships made the greatest gains when they focused on three areas, one of which is structure (the other two are management organization and the manager's leadership abilities). Without a strong relationship structure, your initiative will lack control. Customer satisfaction, communication, and understanding of the business scope will be poor or nonexistent. Technology will most likely be inadequate and the management of the initiative will become reactive rather than proactive.

The first step in structuring the relationship is to define jointly what each of you means when you say you want a good relationship. After that, you need to set the parameters that will help you achieve this good relationship. These parameters can include:

- Metrics and reporting content, calculation, and timing.
- A communication plan and resources for both implementation and steady state.
- Problem resolution and development of steering committee.
- Invoicing format and relevant backup data.

Another parameter is the method you will use to gain consensus. Should all understandings be written to ensure that all involved agree or will implicit understanding work better? You should keep the methodology simple, but make sure it is complete. It is critical that you involve the right people in this process — they should be those people from both companies who can make decisions and accept responsibility for them.

Once you have set these basic parameters, you can determine which structure will work best for you and your outsourcing provider. In the case of logistics outsourcing, there are almost as many relationship structures as there are 3PL agreements; however, the most common types are:

- Dedicated – sole: This is a one-on-one relationship with a provider that has dedicated a warehouse, manufacturing site, or truck fleet to the initiative;
- Dedicated – multiple: This is similar to the dedicated – sole relationship except that it covers several regions or countries, involving more than one warehouse, site, or fleet;
- Multi-client: In a multi-client structure, the provider is operating other contracts under the same roof, co-mingling product in trucks;
- Lead logistics providers (LLPs) — in an LLP structure, one provider takes the lead in the initiative and may manage one or more sub-providers to achieve the client's goals; and
- Formed companies — in this structure, the provider and outsourcer develop a legal entity (company).

The first three types of outsourced logistics structures are self-explanatory and have been around for some time. LLPs and Formed Companies are relatively new and require a little more explanation.

LLPs became popular in the 1990s. An LLP manages all members of its client's supply chain, orchestrating the members' services with their own to meet the client's end objectives. LLPs typically offer process, design, and consulting; expertise on all supply chain elements; all operations and execution; and technology. An LLP is likely to be a 3PL, but consulting firms can be LLPs as well. Their popularity is growing especially in tier one automotive assembly (e.g. Ford Motor Company). A successful LLP can see the big picture and act accordingly. Successful LLPs can collaborate in areas where they may have once competed and have a mix of operations, analytical, and technology skills.

Formed companies are an extension of the LLP concept. Instead of relying on a single, external provider to handle a client's supply chain, formed companies are LLPs that are created from several companies. An example is Vector SCM, a joint venture between General Motors and CNF Company (Menlo Logistics and Trucking), which has hundreds of logisticians, technology engineers, and transportation experts. Vector SCM integrates all of GM's 3PLs under a single umbrella, overseeing GM's supply chain.

The Value of an LLP – Penske Logistics and Whirlpool

In the late 1990s, Whirlpool's senior management conducted an audit of its distribution network. At that time, Whirlpool shared logistics management functions with two incumbent third-party logistics providers, and the audit showed that the company lacked both efficient and consistent logistics processes and procedures. Whirlpool quickly realized they needed a single logistics partner that could identify and remedy inefficiencies up front as well as offer continuous modeling and refining as the distribution network continued to evolve. In November 1998, Whirlpool contracted with Penske Logistics to evaluate and manage its U.S. outbound, finished appliance distribution network.

Using a proven outbound distribution network modeling study, Penske initially determined Whirlpool's complex distribution operations would best be served by a total of eight RDCs and 54 LDCs, representing approximately 3.5 million square feet of space. The development of two additional RDCs were recommended and accepted in one of Penske's subsequent continuous modeling studies. Whirlpool and Penske then worked closely to maximize the use and transition of existing facilities as well as developed new facilities to achieve the optimal network design. RDCs were designed to hold inventory at approximately 59,000 units per month with more than 3,000 different product types on hand. LDCs would not hold inventory, but act as cross-docking facilities instead.

After strategically locating the optimum number of distribution centers strategically throughout the U.S., Penske began work on Whirlpool's transportation network. As part of its agreement with Whirlpool, Penske had acquired Whirlpool's dedicated delivery fleet, known as Quality Express and hired Whirlpool's existing drivers. They retrained them on Penske's streamlined delivery and pick-up procedures. Penske also equipped the fleet with a variety of technological devices, which would enable real-time visibility across the supply chain, such as Qualcomm satellite tracking devices in every power unit and PDAs that capture recipient signatures to confirm receipt of goods and any information regarding damaged freight.

In addition to an optimized distribution and transportation network infrastructure, Penske recommended another strategy for reducing Whirlpool's overall supply chain costs. With an expansive network, Whirlpool could share its network with third-party customers. These customers would not be purchasing major appliances. Rather, Whirlpool could "sell" its distribution and transportation network to other manufacturers who had similar logistics demands. Penske and Whirlpool could work with these third-party customers to maintain inventory and deliver goods. The result would be a new revenue stream, which would reduce the burden of Whirlpool's supply chain costs.

The Penske/Whirlpool partnership has been extremely successful. From 1998 to 2003, the number of Whirlpool appliances shipped per year has increased from 5 million to 9 million and 2,200 Penske employees now run Whirlpool's outbound operations and, most recently, a portion of its inbound operations. This has reduced Whirlpool's overall distribution and transportation costs. As a result, Whirlpool has increased control and visibility over its supply chain, improving accountability throughout the distribution and transportation network. Approximately 99 percent of all orders are delivered on time, while point-of-delivery damages have been reduced by 40 percent. Additionally, Whirlpool realized a 90 percent reduction in inventory shrinkage in 2003.[1]

To determine which of these types of relationships work best for you and your provider, you both must ask some basic questions, such as:

- What is the magnitude of the outsourcing scope-of-work? Is it on the level of running and managing a fleet of trucks, or does it involve an entire distribution or manufacturing network spread all over the world?
- What is the provider's level of experience? Have they basically flown solo or have they worked with several providers on different levels to integrate a supply chain?
- Are you comfortable with "all of our eggs in one basket?" Do you want one outsourcing provider to manage everything or do you want to utilize several providers?
- What is the geography of the outsourcing initiative? Is it nation-wide? Regional? Global?
- Will the outsourcing initiative involve specialization? In other words, are there special requirements involved with the initiative, such as returns, fulfillment, or customer mandates?
- What tasks will the outsourcing provider expect of us? Are we prepared to service their needs?

As you answer these questions, you will begin to get a clearer picture of which type of relationship structure best fits your needs. Below are a few tips for making sure the structure you have identified is successful:

- No matter which structure you choose, you must be very clear about accountability and responsibility. Make sure that both you and your provider understand your roles in the outsourcing initiative and what you expect each other to manage.
- Communicate, communicate, and communicate. We cannot stress enough how important it is for you and your provider to share information openly and honestly. The more each of you knows, the better you can work together within your relationship structure.
- Maximize value for both the client and the outsourcing provider. All participants must win within the structure. Make sure that all parties in the structure will benefit from the relationship. A structure that benefits one participant or a group of participants at the expense of others is a poor structure.
- Company cultures can be everything. It is important that each company understands the other's culture and that both can work

in harmony so that the relationship structure can evolve. As a result, trust will grow as expectations are met. Open discussions about trust are to be encouraged.

Once you and your provider have determined your relationship structure and taken the first steps toward ensuring that your relationship is based on trust, the next step is to establish the fee structure for the initiative. Putting a pricing structure in place is an important relationship hurdle.

SELECTING A FEE STRUCTURE

The fee structure for an outsourcing initiative serves as the basis for the service agreement between an outsourcer and a provider. Often, an outsourcer will have a pre-conceived notion of fee structure and will not give a provider the latitude to develop the most beneficial approach. This is a mistake. The best fee structures are developed mutually after the parties have explored all the possibilities. Otherwise, you may wind up with a fee structure that is too rigid and does not allow for the changes inherent in a long-term outsourcing relationship. Fee structures should be as flexible as the relationships that create them.

At the highest level the pricing (fee) options are:

- Fixed-cost
- Transactional fee
- Cost-plus
- Activity-based
- Management fee
- Combined structures

Each option has advantages and disadvantages. It is important that both you and your provider explore each option before you decide which you will apply to your outsourcing initiative. Your goal is to develop the structure that works best for your solution. The sections that follow discuss the structures in more depth.

Fixed-cost Fee Structure

This fee structure works best when the outsourcing initiative involves predictable volumes. It in its simplest form, the provider agrees to do the work for a set price rather than being paid on a time and materials basis. A more complex form (although it is still simpler than other models) is a service level-driven, fixed-cost agreement ("fixed-price SLA"). In this case, the provider must meet predetermined performance levels before they can realize any revenue.

Fixed-cost fee structures have several benefits. For example, it is difficult to misinterpret a fixed price. In fact, the pricing is easy to understand and it simplifies the client's budgeting process.

The disadvantages are that when providers determine their fixed fees, they are prone to overestimating their costs to minimize their risk and guarantee that their fixed costs will be covered. Also, if wages are involved, they can rise over time, creating the possibility that the provider will lose money.

Transactional Fee Structure

The transactional fee structure is the most common pricing model. Most public warehouses and a number of dedicated 3PLs use this approach to pricing. Basically, a flat fee is charged per unit cost of work, such as miles driven, pallets handled, and cases merchandized. For example, a transactional fee structure for outsourcing transportation might include a cost per mile, a labor charge per hour, a charge per door shunt, and a trailer per day fee.

The transactional fee structure offers several advantages. Like the fixed-cost model, it simplifies budgeting because the client knows in advance what the provider's services will cost. Also, it is easy to understand because each item is broken down into a dollar amount. Invoicing is easy because the provider can submit invoices based on the charges determined before work starts. Finally, there are industry benchmarks for most costing so the client can be sure that the provider's fees are reasonable and fair.

The disadvantages include:

- It is difficult for providers to cover their fixed costs when this structure is used because costs are based on workloads that vary with volume;
- The outsourcer can end up paying too much if the rates are not based on reasonable time estimates to perform each function;
- The costing is based solely on volume, when in fact other variables such as fixed costs for utilities and fuel don't vary based on volume;
- The elements in the costing structure are unclear and too much is left open to interpretation; and
- It is a commodity approach rather than a partnering approach.

Cost-plus Fee Structure

This pricing option is the actual cost of the initiative plus a percentage fee or flat fee (Figure 1). It is especially effective if your outsourcing project is volatile and is less likely to be applied to a long-term initiative. The cost-plus fee structure is popular with large providers, mainly because they will make money in every circumstance. In some cases, a provider may mandate that this model be used.

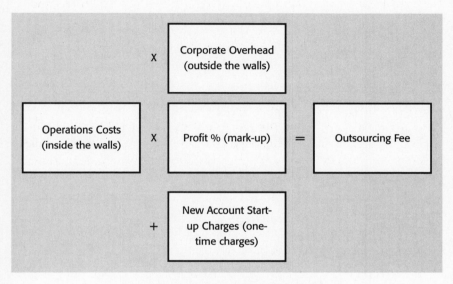

Figure 1. The Cost-plus Pricing Model

For example, consider a warehousing outsourcing project. Using the cost-plus model, the following would be included in the operational costs: staff, management, equipment, facility, consumables, communication, and hardware/software costs. Included in corporate overhead would be IT, accounting, EDI, customer service, sales, and senior management costs. The one-time costs in the new account start-up block would be engineering and logistics design, travel, systems integration and communications, leasehold agreements, and capital requirements costs.

This fee structure has a number of advantages, which is why it is popular. A key benefit of the cost-plus structure is that it can be combined with other fee structures. Another advantage is that it builds trust between a provider and a client as they work out all the costs and "do the math." Clients will have an accurate picture of costs and providers will have a picture of their profits, which are guaranteed even when the unexpected happens. Cost-plus also improves start-up when a costing structure is unclear, eliminates contingency padding, and, if volumes fluctuate or are not easily defined, the provider is not at risk. At the same time, clients do not feel that they are overpaying and they perceive the structure as innovative and flexible.

The disadvantages of this type of fee structure are:

- The provider must be able to capture costs accurately. This includes understanding the base for overhead and an allocation formula, or understanding that engineering standards should be a part of engineering costs. Otherwise, costs that should be taken into consideration may be overlooked or priced incorrectly;
- There is often a perception among outsourcers that this structure provides no built-in motivation for the provider to reduce costs and improve productivity without including incentives for reducing costs and enhancing service;
- Disagreements on what constitutes a cost can arise; and
- Budgeting is more difficult for the client because the only constant is the markup.

The cost-plus fee structure also has a major impact on the service agreement. Clients must audit costs and conduct budget reviews (yearly or even quarterly). Also, there is a sliding index on overhead markups that relates to revenue profit mark-up on start-up costs.

Activity-Based Fee Structure

This hybrid fee structure includes a flat fee component and a transactional fee component. If the provider you selected is a 3PL, the flat fee components are building space, equipment depreciation, and equipment leases. The transactional fee is based on volume and covers those costs that vary for the provider such as labor, maintenance, and fuel.

The advantages of this fee structure are similar to those of cost-plus pricing. It can protect a provider when volume is unpredictable. Also, the provider is more likely to charge a fair price because they do not feel obliged to "fatten" their unit prices to protect themselves from losses related to their fixed costs. It also more accurately reflects services rendered and expenses incurred and allows clients and providers to track logistics costs more accurately because they usually have more highly detailed invoices.

Like the benefits, the disadvantages for activity-based fee structures resemble those for cost-plus. Their pricing structures are complex to develop and there are no inherent financial incentives for the providers to pursue continuous improvement. Also, activity-based pricing is difficult to structure for new relationships since there might be many unknowns.

Management Fee Cost Structure

The management fee pricing model is structured as a fixed annual charge for required services. In a few cases, it includes all elements of the agreement, including direct costs, overhead and fixed cost, and profit. Typically, however, the client is responsible for direct costs as they are billed and a set management fee is used to cover the provider's overhead and profit.

Like the activity-based and cost-plus models, the management fee structure can be combined with other fee structures and is a viable option for projects where units are not easily defined and volume and shipping levels are speculative. Other advantages include fewer disagreements over operating charges and service levels than with other structures, improved management productivity, and fixed provider profit and overhead.

The problems with this structure include no set method of passing along productivity gains. Also, setting the appropriate fee may be problematic. Like all the other fee structures, there are no built-in motivators to improve effectiveness nor is there incentive for the provider to expand needed supervisory/management efforts.

Combined Structures

Many fee structures developed between clients and providers are combinations of several structures. It is fairly common for a pricing model to be a combination of the transaction, cost-plus, and management fee structures. For example, an East Coast company may have a remote operation in California in which it pays a third party to ship goods to its West Coast customers on a per-unit basis. However, it also has a main facility operated by a third party. The East Coast company owns the facility and the product, but the employees work for the third party. In this case, the company pays the 3PL a management fee to operate the facility and the 3PL bills the company for expenses as they accrue. A few states away, another third party operates a facility for the East Coast company and is paid on a cost-plus basis. The third party bills the company for all the costs, which also pays a percentage fee to the provider for its profit and overhead.

There are other possible, successful combinations of fee structures that you may use if you choose. Of course, what is best will always be debated and is an interesting subject of conversation in each outsourcing relationship. For example, some industry insiders will tell you that you should never use cost-plus, yet in a situation where there are too many unknowns or your business processes are changing radically, a cost-plus structure works well. Once your processes become more stable or after the initiative has been underway for some time, you may want to revisit the fee structure and make mutually agreed upon modifications. Or you may find that you don't need to make any adjustments at all.

What is important is that you and your provider explore all the pricing possibilities and their ramifications before you settle on a fee structure. You both should keep in mind that what worked best for one provider-client relationship, even if that relationship involved one or both of you, may not be best for this particular initiative. Pricing, at best, is a difficult subject, but if you and your provider approach it with open minds and a view toward flexibility, as well as full disclosure and no assumptions, together you can find the right approach.

Once you have determined which fee structure to use, you can begin discussions about how to build in improvement factors. As you may have noticed as you read the disadvantages of the various structures, most of them do not have inherent, built-in measures for encouraging continuous improvement, enhanced service, or cost reduction. At this stage, you want to approach the concept cautiously; however, it is important that both you and the provider discuss your joint expectations of the potential for continuous improvement and fee structure. Then, you will be ready for the next step in the process of creating your relationship: validation or relationship due diligence.

Controversial Issue – Risk vs. Reward

Most service agreements have penalties built into them to protect the client. In many cases, this creates a win-lose situation, where the client is temporarily the winner. However, in the long run, if you only penalize your provider, you will lose because the provider will have no incentive to exceed service levels or develop innovative, cost-reducing strategies. To truly make the relationship between partner and provider a win-win, both parties in the relationship must benefit when things go well. Therefore, a wise client with an eye towards a successful outsourcing initiative will build in a risk-for-reward structure.

At Tompkins Associates, when we make this suggestion, we often get asked, "Why reward the provider for something I am paying for and expect them to deliver?" The point is that you do not reward them for delivery, but for exceeding expectations and continuous improvement. Rewards can include bonus payments, increased profit margins, or some form of a gain-sharing/pain-sharing or goal-sharing process. You should discuss these during the process of determining your fee structure and make sure that a reward that all parties agree is win-win is selected.

VALIDATION (RELATIONSHIP DUE DILIGENCE)

Consider this situation. After an exhaustive review of responses to RFIs and RFPs, Company A selected Provider X to operate several DCs. Provider X had impeccable financials; its records showed a strong, solvent company with the latest software, and according to its references, its employees were well-trained. Site visits to other DCs managed by Provider X revealed efficient operations. So, Company A entered into an agreement with Provider X. In the end, however, Company A's outsourcing initiative failed. Why? Because Company A made false assumptions about Provider X based on what they read and saw. Yes, Provider X had the latest software, but unfortunately, its IT staff did not know how to install it on Company A's legacy systems. Provider X's operations were efficient because of well-defined processes and methodologies; however, the company did not know how to apply those processes and methodologies in Company A's DC.

This story illustrates one of life's lessons: "What looks good on paper doesn't necessarily work well in real life." Provider X looked like the perfect candidate to Company A. However, real life revealed otherwise. What both companies should have done, before signing any agreements, was go through a validation process, often called relationship due diligence. Had they done this, Company A may have realized that it needed to upgrade its legacy systems or Provider X might have hired personnel who had experience installing up-to-date software on older systems. Had Provider X discussed Company A's DC operations before signing the agreement, they might have realized that the processes needed an overhaul before their workforce took over.

During validation, a client and a provider work together as a team to understand what the other is selling and what it needs. Both must be prepared to change assumptions or make adjustments to their expectations. A provider should take the RFP and make sure the client clarifies it. The provider should ask probing questions and work toward a more granular level of detail than the RFP provides. In turn, you should ask your provider for detailed data analysis and ask revealing questions about their proposed solution. During this process, you should also assess your organizations' cultural fit, identifying differing philosophies and determining how to make them work or how to overcome them.

Once the validation process is complete, you and the provider can create a timeline.

SETTING REALISTIC TIMELINE EXPECTATIONS

Before you and your provider get involved in the legal issues necessary for cementing your relationship, you need to develop a realistic and detailed timeline. Below is a list of dates you should determine together:

- Due Diligence complete
- Term sheet signing
- Service Agreement signing
- Communication plan — internal
- Communication plan — customers, vendors
- Resource assessment
- Create project teams
- Regulatory issues
- Transition planning
- Operations planning
- Technology planning
- Benchmarking
- New equipment/facilities acquisition
- News releases
- Go-live dates
- HR issues
- Training
- Testing
- Inventory planning — product movement plans

Creating the Outsource Relationship: Two-Provider Strategy

During a provider selection several years ago, Tompkins Associates began creating the outsource relationship with two potential providers. We informed both providers that we wanted to go through the process of creating relationships with both of them. We followed the steps outlined in this chapter with both providers, including fee structure selection and due diligence. We also developed term sheets and transition plans with both.

During this process we were able to eliminate one of the providers after we realized that they were struggling with the level of detail that creating a relationship entails and that they also had trouble being flexible on key issues.

This strategy creates an opportunity to try out a provider for a period of time before making a final decision — much like test driving two cars to determine which one best meets your needs. It has been used by Toyota and other companies for many years to gain an understanding of provider's capabilities before putting too much at risk. It is not for the faint of heart because it can be expensive in terms of time and resources, but it is a good strategy if done properly.

Discussing the elements listed above and the key dates of the initiative creates common thinking about the process and the next steps. It will also result in the outline of what will become your outsourcing plan. Once this is accomplished, you are ready to concentrate on forging a legal relationship with your provider, which is the subject of the next chapter.

---

1 Penske Logistics, "What If Your Customers Chose On Supply Chain Efficiency — Would You Win?" Whirlpool Case Study, 2004, http://www.penskelogistics.com/casestudies/whirlpool.html

ON THE ELEVATOR

Outsourcing is giving up internal control of a business function and trusting others to handle this function for you. Therefore, the relationship between you and your outsourcing provider cannot be taken lightly. Although you may have built a great relationship during the selection process, this is not the outsourcing relationship that will take you through your initiative. Creating the outsourcing relationship involves:

- Getting the relationship started — A failed relationship can lead to complicated and costly legal battles. Therefore, as soon as is practicable, you should create a new team — the implementation team — comprised of members of both companies to begin the process of creating your relationship. This includes setting initial expectations, identifying resources in advance, determining where you are now and your destination, defining the relationship desired, and planning for resistance.
- Determining the relationship structure — Structure is important. Without a strong relationship structure, your initiative will lack control. Customer satisfaction, communication, and understanding of the business scope will be poor or nonexistent. Technology will most likely be inadequate and the management of the initiative will become reactive rather than proactive. Therefore, once you have started your relationship, you must determine what structure will work best.
- Selecting a fee structure — Fee structures should be as flexible as the relationships that create them. At the highest level, the pricing (fee) options are: fixed-cost, transactional fee, cost-plus, activity-based, management fee, and combined

structures. Each option has advantages and disadvantages. It is important that both you and your provider explore each option before you decide which you will apply to your initiative.

- Validation (relationship due diligence) — During validation, a client and a provider work together as a team to understand what the other is selling and what it needs. Both must be prepared to change assumptions or make adjustments to their expectations.
- Setting realistic timeline expectations — Before you and your provider get involved in the legal issues necessary for cementing your relationship, you need to develop a realistic and detailed timeline. This creates common thinking about the process and the next steps.

This process is not always going to be perfect, but there are a few things you can keep in mind as you work together to help it along:

- Do not over-promise on either side;
- Share information;
- Analyze available data, understand that it is likely to be historical, and deal with data gaps and integrity;
- Tour sites to see them with your own eyes;
- Do not make unfounded assumptions; and
- Line up all levels and functional groups from both organizations.

Most importantly, make sure that you ask a lot of questions and encourage the provider to do the same. Although this is not rocket science, it is complex. The more questions you ask and answer, the better off your relationship will be.

Successful Outsourcing Relationships: A Legal Perspective

INTRODUCTION

This chapter can be summed up with a simple maxim: *Involve experienced outsource legal counsel early.* Nearly every high-level commentary written on the subject of outsourcing has as its central theme the critical need to develop a true partnership between the parties. Commentators use catchy phrases like "developing a partnership mindset," "cultivating a common culture," or striving for the ubiquitous "win-win" scenario. In other words, the often repeated admonition to view the outsource relationship as a partnership is a bedrock principal. A successful outsourcing relationship is like any successful marriage, business partnership, joint venture, and social or religious organization; it is a relationship of mutual benefit and dependence.

The idea of nurturing such a relationship into being is almost antithetical, however, to the heavy handedness typical of contract negotiations. Lawyers are not wedding planners or marriage counselors. Instead, through prenuptial agreements, lawyers plan for the divorce before the rings are exchanged. As advocates, lawyers look to seize the advantages and exploit the weaknesses in relationships. They understand that the concept of unconscionable terms rarely exists between two commercial parties. Moreover, the risk-shifting role of the advocate and the midwife role of the relationship builder are seemingly dichotomous.

Counsel experienced in outsourcing issues, with knowledge of a company's business, a thorough understanding of the motives behind the decision to outsource, and an appreciation of the synergies between service user and service provider, can guide a company successfully through contract negotiations without poisoning the relationship. Experienced counsel understands that the ultimate goal is a successful outsourcing

relationship and that this is achieved only with a fair and balanced allocation of risk, regardless of how much leverage one side may possess
during and after negotiations. Finally, while understanding the need for
a contractual foundation on which the parties can cultivate a common
culture, experienced counsel knows that the relationship is not a true
legal partnership (even though the parties involved may refer to themselves as partners and try to treat one another as such) and will not
lose sight of the need to protect the client and the client's assets from
unnecessary risk.

Interestingly, the better that your company and your provider do at
forming a legal relationship, the less likely it is needed. If the legal relationship is well formed, the success of the relationship will be measured
by the accomplishment of the goals established for the outsourcing initiative. But if you have done poorly in forging the legal relationship, the
more it is actually needed. And the protection that the legal relationship
provides each of the parties will be the criteria used to determine how
poorly the relationship was crafted.

To form a strong, mutually beneficial and successful legal relationship,
you need the assistance of experienced legal counsel and, as stated at the
beginning of this chapter, that assistance is needed early in the process.
What is often surprising therefore, is how often outsourcing relationships
and initiatives are created without the benefit of counsel at all. This chapter stresses not only the importance of involving experienced counsel in
the outsourcing process, but also the importance of involving counsel
early. It also addresses the components of forging a strong, successful
legal relationship between you and your providers, including negotiation
strategies, contract terms, and binding versus nonbinding contracts.

INVOLVING COUNSEL

It is critical to the success of your outsourcing venture that you include
experienced legal counsel on your outsourcing team. This should be a
"no-brainer." Yet, many companies do not understand this and enter
into the contracting and negotiation process with outsourcing providers
without the benefit of legal guidance. This is a recipe for failure. There
are pitfalls and risks in the process of selecting and contracting with an
outsourcing provider — pitfalls and risks that you may not even consider
because you do not have the experience to consider them. Experienced
counsel can navigate you through the muddy waters and help you achieve

the outsourcing relationship that will best benefit your company. If you do not have an in-house legal team, seek the advice of experienced outside counsel.

When to Involve Counsel: Old Dogs Can Learn New Tricks

Tompkins Associates performed its first outsourcing project 20 years ago, and our first consulting assignment for an outsource provider was 15 years ago. Ten years ago, we benchmarked our outsource consulting offerings against our competition. We had a very competitive offering with several distinct features not provided by our competition. Our outsourcing practice was strong, profitable and growing. Our outsourcing process and methodologies were well defined and robust.

Imagine our surprise, then, when five years ago we began to see a significant percentage of outsourcing deals that were going bad. As we identified one of the key reasons deals were going bad, we realized that it was something that we too were not doing well. Fortunately, none of our deals had gone bad, but the reality was that we had a hole in our process. We fixed this hole, but, interestingly, in the majority of outsource relationships today, it is still a huge hole in the outsource consulting support offered by most consulting firms.

What is this huge outsourcing hole? Simply put, it is not involving legal representation in the development of the outsourcing relationship early in the process and keeping counsel involved throughout the process. When we compare the outsourcing work we did five years ago with the outsourcing work we provide now, there simply is no comparison. Our prior process did well in RFP development, but relied very heavily on the workings of the client and provider during and after implementation to truly define the outsource relationship. Because of this, it is unclear that we always selected the right provider.

Recently, we decided to involve our legal team in the RFI, RFP, and selection process. The selection process resulted in two finalists, The Best and Second Best. Obviously, The Best came out of the selection process in the lead to win this business. When the legal team took the lead in parallel negotiation with these two firms on a Term Sheet, however, The Best firm adopted a hard-ball stance and in relatively short order disqualified itself from the competition. Second Best, by contrast, was firm, but fair and open. A successful Term Sheet, Agreement, relationship, and working partnership evolved from this process. Without doubt, if a "standard" contract had been put in place with The Best, the result would have been a failed relationship. Getting legal involved early brought this realization to the surface.

"How could this happen? The selection process must have been flawed," is the general reaction to this example. Well, first, the selection process was not flawed. The difference was that, at The Best, there was one team that "sold" the engagement and another that "worked" the engagement. So, when legal took the lead on the Term Sheet, the team at The Best changed out and an aggressive, macho attitude came forth. We were surprised because we had met the execution team during the sales process and they had appeared to be easy going and quiet. But once they were positioned to take the lead, they began to demonstrate how they really would be as partners. By contrast, at Second Best, the sales team consisted of several people from the execution team.

Because we had involved legal early, we helped a client avoid a major mistake. So, although we have been doing outsourcing for over 20 years (old dogs) we have continued to learn how to improve this process (new tricks).

It is also crucial that you involve counsel early in the process. Your counsel needs time to understand the drivers behind your decision to outsource and whether the motivation to outsource is to focus on core competency; reduce cost; acquire best of breed technology or processes; free up capital; or some or all of these motives. To further the relationship building process, your counsel must understand the synergies between you and your provider or providers, how motives are aligned, what the expectations are at the outset, and the criteria for success.

The above requirements dictate early and thorough involvement. Some companies may want counsel present when they identify core competencies to help the legal team gain the understanding of their motivations for outsourcing. Others might bring in legal when they are drafting the RFI and searching for recipients of the RFPs. The very latest in the process that you should bring in legal counsel is before you draft the RFP, but it is to your advantage not to wait that long. Involving the legal team in creating the RFI improves your selection process dramatically because your counsel will be familiar with all the players and can contribute to the selection process. This also better prepares the legal team when it is time to negotiate, which is the subject of the next section.

NEGOTIATION STRATEGIES

Your legal team's outsourcing negotiation strategies should include understanding your company's negotiating position and objectives in the outsourcing initiative. To accomplish this, make sure your counsel has the answers to the following questions:

- What is driving the decision to outsource — commercial, financial, technological?
- What departments are impacted and what are the consequences to each?
- How can the objectives be utilized in negotiations with the provider?

Also, if you did not involve legal in the development of the scope of services that meets your objectives, make sure that you share the scope of services at this point.

You and your legal team should also decide whether to wait until you have selected one final provider (sole source) before you start the negotiations or to begin the negotiation process with two finalists (negotiating in parallel). The benefits of negotiating in parallel include:

- Leverage — nothing will make a vendor sharpen his focus more than a competition;
- The best price;
- Disclosure of misunderstandings regarding the requirements and expectations through price mismatches;
- Exposure to alternative technical and commercial solutions;
- More flexible terms and conditions; and
- The best approach to handling change.

As the "old dogs learn new tricks" story illustrated, negotiating in parallel may even bring into stark contrast the differences between your two finalists or reveal less than desirable characteristics that might not have emerged if the company had been approached after selection. This is yet another benefit.

Negotiating in parallel is not without its cons, however. The more obvious drawbacks are that it increases costs and time and requires more team members to manage the negotiation. Also, often a single supplier will have a clear and insurmountable advantage, thereby negating the benefits of competitive procurement. A more subtle detriment is the effect it can have on your relationship with whichever provider you select. Basically, playing one provider off another is not conducive to achieving the partnership mindset that must be cultivated from the initial contact.

Whether you decide to negotiate with one provider or two, your legal relationship can take several paths during negotiations. Some of the options include:

- Binding term sheet to contract;
- Letter of intent or non-binding term sheet to contract;
- Letter of intent to binding term sheet to contract; and
- Contract.

The provider you have selected may try to influence you toward taking the contract path. Most providers are looking for assurance that your company will not abandon them in the middle of the initiative and will be eager to negotiate long-term contracts (five years or more). The problem with this is that the current business climate is so dynamic that companies cannot make forecasts beyond one or two years, and it is rare for anyone to know where their company will be in five years.

Because business continues to change at a faster rate than ever before, it is recommended that you lead the negotiations with a binding term sheet, which allows you to settle on the terms of the deal without bogging down the parties involved in "legalese." If the term sheet is comprehensive and properly negotiated, there is little reason to make it nonbinding. Letters of intent are usually nonbinding because they lack substance. Ultimately, the schedule is the determining factor. A binding term sheet is necessary where long lead items like site selection, equipment sourcing, and IT integration must be initiated in order to meet the schedule.

The negotiated term sheet embodies the deal and will be the basis of the agreement. Properly constructed, it makes preparation, negotiation, and execution of the definitive agreement a simple process and allows you to continue to evaluate and improve the service provider's proposed charges, technical solutions, and legal terms.

Ideally, your term sheet should cover everything. For example, it should not differentiate between legal and business issues because nearly all issues are business issues. However, at minimum, the term sheet must:

- Integrate commercial, legal, technical, and financial issues;
- Balance risk and reward;
- Balance certainty and flexibility;
- Provide price predictability;
- Plan for exit.

The next section discusses specific contract terms to be included in the term sheet. Once they are outlined in the term sheet, your legal team can build on them for the actual contract or service agreement.

CONTRACT TERMS

Negotiating an outsourcing term sheet (or agreement or contract) differs from negotiating routine purchase or service agreements because they usually involve intellectual property, warranties, creative design, epidemic failure, liability, and indemnity provisions. Therefore, the contact terms for your initiative may not resemble other term sheets or contracts you have seen in the past. This section identifies outsourcing contract terms, all of which should be included in the term sheet and executed in the final agreement.

The contract terms that will be the subject of a great deal of discussion between your company, the legal team, and the provider are *service levels* and *performance measures*. The service level part of the agreement must identify each service level clearly and objectively while making sure that those services that are inappropriate for service levels are clearly defined, measurable, and achievable, as well. Service levels are the mechanisms for enabling the measurement of performance and are often linked to service response times, system performance times, and fix times for faults. When you and your counsel are negotiating service levels, you should pay particular attention to those service levels that will affect the organization's core functions and its prime business indicators and how you will determine whether they have been achieved.

The failure to achieve service levels can lead to service credits, which are created when the provider does not meet any of the individual performance standards for the service levels set forth in this section. In order to be enforceable, these should be a reasonable pre-estimate of the loss that will be suffered as a result of the failure to achieve the service level. At the same time, you will want to consider whether these service credits should be an exclusive remedy or whether, in addition to any service credits that may be gained, an aggrieved customer can also make a claim in damages or terminate the agreement.

Performance measures are usually included with service levels, and you and your provider must agree on them prior to signing an agreement. These should be clear, objective Key Performance Indicators (KPI) that are aligned with your strategic direction, are appropriate to the project, and provide readily understood signals of when the provider is succeeding and when improvement is needed. The KPIs for a distribution center, for example, might include measured customer satisfaction, on-time delivery performance, inventory accuracy, on-time receipt performance, and so forth.

The metrics will vary, depending on the tasks that your provider will perform. A common practice is to include a provision for benchmarks against which you and your provider periodically compare services and prices with industry best practices. This requires looking outside your organization for best-in-class performance comparisons and comparing your business with companies within and outside your industry. Many consulting groups and research organizations have developed formal benchmarking data and offer it as a product for this purpose. Once the metrics are collected, a gap analysis is completed that typically looks at the best-in-class performer within and outside of your industry. This is followed by more analysis to assess the degree to which actual practice changes are necessary to approach or achieve these levels.

Value-Based Benchmarking: Soleus Group

The most comprehensive and relevant supply chain benchmarking methodology that Tompkins Associates has experienced is Value-Based Benchmarking℠ provided by Soleus Group, a consulting services company focused on assisting its clients in achieving world-class supply chain execution. Participating companies are able to compare their operations to their peers, to best practices and to emerging supply chain innovations. Value-Based Benchmarking establishes a baseline for capturing performance measures relevant to an organization's processes, systems, and organization. Using this baseline, Soleus clients and partners can set improvement targets and measure progress.

Value-Based Benchmarking focuses on the questions, trends, and performance measures that ultimately lead to superior financial performance and good corporate citizenship. It is based on a unique, globally focused repository of supply chain best practices. To ensure the repository is vital and relevant, content is driven by steering committees led by senior representatives from shippers, carriers, and other logistics service providers. The content is detailed and actionable and includes operational processes, performance metrics, trends, priorities and organizational profiles.

The best practice repository is built through a process that includes developing surveys, collecting data from participants, interpreting results with the participants, and summarizing conclusions and insights. Select functional areas in each industry are reviewed on a rotating basis so that information remains current.

The best practices content spans a broad range of strategic and tactical supply chain capabilities. On a tactical or execution level, functional capabilities from order creation through order delivery and receipt are covered. Participant involvement below the senior management level is organized by function to make data collection and analysis more manageable.

Some of the functional breakdowns include:

- Order Management
- International Operations
- Truck Transportation
- Ocean Transportation
- Fleet Management
- Technology
- Distribution Center Operations
- Organization and Budget
- Inventory Management

By participating in the Value-Based Benchmarking process, companies gain insights from "companies like us". This encourages breakout discovery and revolutionizes improvement opportunities.

Once you and your provider have discussed and established service levels and performance metrics, you can discuss the other terms of your agreement, which include:

- Term — This sets forth the length of the agreement. Usually, the initial term, which is the actual length of the agreement, is mentioned first and followed by an extension term that addresses the issue of renewing the agreement.
- Schedule — This section of the agreement describes the key dates for the project.

- Scope of services — This is the section of the agreement that spells out exactly what the outsourcer will be doing for your company. For example, the scope of services for a logistics agreement can include: transition services (the activities that facilitate the transition of the outsourced process from your company to theirs such as facility and software upgrades, equipment installation, hiring and training personnel, and testing and upgrading systems), general warehousing services, additional warehousing services, and value-added services.

- Price — This is the part of the agreement that discusses the price of the provider's services and the type of pricing arrangement between the two parties.

- Payment terms — In this section of the agreement, the method of payment is described. It establishes the invoice terms and the payment terms. It should also create a clear understanding of how these issues will change and evolve over the life of the relationship.

- Ownership and confidentiality of data — This section clearly delineates who owns intellectual rights to data and other proprietary information and that all data and information will remain confidential and will not be shared with parties outside the agreement.

- Governance — This spells out who will have ultimate responsibility over the agreement and who will have the authority to make decisions regarding the initiative. It also addresses issue escalation.

- Insurance requirements — This part of the agreement delineates the various types of insurance the outsourcer is expected to provide your company and the amounts of the coverage.

- Staffing — This section identifies the provider's primary representative as well as key personnel on the project. It discusses the relationships between your company and the provider and describes how to handle subcontractors and other human resource issues.

- Performance incentives — This is the section for detailing rewards for exceeding service levels or not meeting them. Commonly included in this part of the term sheet and agreement is a performance bond. Incentives are not as common; however, rewarding the provider for going above and beyond service levels is appropriate and fosters the relationship.

- Business recovery — This section covers the disaster recovery plan the provider will put in place, the date that it will be in place, and the terms of its periodic review and testing.
- Representations and warranties — Representations are statements of past and existing facts, and warranties are promises that existing or future facts are or will be true. Representations and warranties may relate to financial information, taxes, contracts, intellectual property, benefits, and so on, covering virtually every business aspect. In an outsourcing agreement, the standard representations and warranties for both the outsourcing provider and the client state that their companies are in good standing, that they have the power to enter into the contract, that they have not defaulted on other contracts or judgments, and that there are no pending judgments or judicial or administrative orders against them except as disclosed in the agreement. This is also the part of the agreement where it is stated that when the term sheet is properly executed, it will be a valid and binding obligation.
- Warranty of services — This is the part of the agreement where the provider will promise that it can and will deliver the services and products on schedule in a diligent and workmanlike manner in accordance with professional standards. The outsourcer also states that its service will meet or exceed the service levels described in the agreement and will be delivered by qualified personnel.
- Non-solicitation of employees — This part of the agreement is where both parties agree not to try to hire an employee of the other party away from the current employer or convince one to leave his or her employer. In some agreements, the companies might clarify the position of the employee that may not be solicited, such as a supervisor or manager.
- Audit — This section sets forth the audit rights for the outsourcing initiative. In it, the provider agrees to allow, upon prior written notice (the period is also determined in this section) your company auditors access to facilities to evaluate the outsourcer's performance and to assure that the outsourcer is complying with the agreement. It also states how frequently the audits will occur, who can be an auditor, what records must be retained for use during the audits, that the outsourcer will cooperate during the audit, and what to do if an audit determines that the outsourcer has overcharged you.

- Liquidated damages — In this part of the agreement, you and the outsourcer state what compensation your company will receive from the provider should they fail to meet their obligations (such as schedule and services) and it is determined that this failure was not caused by your company's actions. In some agreements, the client might also use this section to indicate that the compensation outlined in this section is all the client will seek from the outsourcer.

- Indemnification — This is the contractual obligation of each company to "hold harmless" the other company from losses caused by any willful misconduct or illegal actions on their part. In this section of the agreement, you and the provider agree not to hold the other liable for willful misconduct or illegal actions and also agree to the extent to which you are obligated to each other should legal action be required.

- Limitation of liability — Because an outsourcing provider usually has access to (and often responsibility for) your product, this also makes them liable for your product. This portion of the term sheet, agreement, or contract spells out the outsourcer's liability in terms of your product as well as in terms of its promise to provide services at levels and adhere to the schedule described in the service agreement.

- Dispute resolution — During the selection phase when all parties are on their best behavior, it is difficult to imagine that there will be any disputes that can't be resolved with a meeting and a handshake. Unfortunately, that rosy view can deteriorate quickly after a provider is selected and the work begins, and this is when your counsel takes on the role of an attorney drafting a pre-nuptial agreement for a newly engaged couple. This part of the agreement should clearly identify the steps that will be taken to resolve disputes between both companies that have been escalated above operational and executive levels before, during, and after the dispute has reached binding, non-appealing arbitration.

- Termination and termination assistance — Again, this is another part of the outsourcing agreement that the engaged couple or newlyweds do not like to contemplate. It describes how and why each party can terminate the agreement, how the party terminating the agreement will compensate the other, and how termination assistance will be provided should the outsourcer terminate the agreement.

- Assignability/right to subcontract — Many providers rely on subcontractors for certain services. This section of the term sheet, agreement, or contract is where you should state whether or not the provider can use subcontractors. If so, you should state the procedures to be followed, including when and how you are notified and your right to approve or disallow their sub-contracts.
- Governing law — With today's global economy, it is likely that you and your provider may not be headquartered in the same state or even in the same hemisphere. This section identifies the laws of the states and countries that will govern the agreement and, in particular, any arbitration involved in dispute resolution.

For each portion of the agreement mentioned above, it is important that you, your counsel, and the provider expend energy to ensure that everything is clearly stated and that all issues are understood. Make sure that you include the details and schedule for transition steps. Key questions that need to be answered include:

- What assets, operations, employees, testing and go-live transition steps need to take place and who has responsibility and accountability for these to happen?
- What will take place if these do not happen as planned?
- How will you know if these transition steps occurred or not?

Once you have done this, all parties will have a solid foundation for drafting the final contract and executing the service agreement. Then, it is time to put the outsourcing relationship into motion (see Chapter 10).

ON THE ELEVATOR

Involve experienced outsource counsel early. Your legal team needs time to understand the drivers behind your decision to outsource and what your goals are for the outsourcing initiative. It is best to involve the legal team before or during the RFI step to improve your selection process. Your counsel will then be familiar with all the players and can contribute to the selection process. This also better prepares the legal team when it is time to negotiate.

Your legal team's outsourcing negotiation strategies should include understanding your company's negotiating position and objectives in the outsourcing initiative. To accomplish this, make sure your counsel has the answers to the following questions:

• What is driving the decision to outsource — commercial, financial, technological?
• What departments are impacted and what are the consequences to each?
• How can the objectives be utilized in negotiations with the provider?

You and your legal team should also decide whether to wait until you have selected one final provider (sole source) before you start the negotiations or to begin the negotiation process with two finalists (negotiating in parallel).

It is best to lead the negotiations with a binding term sheet, which allows you to settle on the terms of the deal without bogging down the parties involved in "legalese." The negotiated term sheet embodies the deal and will be the basis of the agreement. Properly constructed, it makes preparation, negotiation, and execution of the definitive agreement a simple process and allows you to continue to evaluate and improve the service provider's proposed charges, technical solutions, and legal terms:

At minimum, the term sheet must:

• Integrate commercial, legal, technical, and financial issues;
• Balance risk and reward;
• Balance certainty and flexibility;
• Provide price predictability;
• Plan for exit.

The contract terms that will be the subject of a great deal of discussion between your company, the legal team, and the provider are service levels and performance measures. The service level part of the agreement must identify each service level clearly and objectively. Performance measures are usually included with service levels. These are performance indicators that are aligned with your strategic direction, are appropriate to the project, and provide readily understood signals of when the provider is succeeding and when improvement is needed. A common practice is to include a provision for benchmarks against which you and your provider periodically compare services and prices with industry best practices. This requires looking outside your organization for best-in-class performance comparisons and comparing your business with companies within and outside your industry. Many consulting groups and research organizations have developed formal benchmarking data and offer it as a product for this purpose.

For each portion of the term sheet, it is important that you, your counsel, and the provider expend energy to make sure everything is clearly stated and that all issues are understood. Once you have done this, all parties will have a solid foundation for drafting the final contract and executing the service agreement.

Getting Started: Putting the Outsourcing Relationship in Motion

INTRODUCTION

Although outsourcing is currently very popular, many companies continue to debate whether or not to outsource operations. Those in the "not outsource category" continually say that providers always underperform, there are no savings, and that they have never seen a provider work towards continuous improvement at any level. Certainly, there are many examples of these comments being true, and it seems that there are as many outsourcing failures as there are successes. Interestingly, most of these failures occur in the early stages of the initiative, particularly during start-up. There are several reasons for this.

Failure during start-up can often be attributed to a changing of the guard from the provider's sales team to their account management team. Although this is normal and a good practice, the skill set and focus are often different. This is not to say that the sales team will disappear; however, they will take a sideline seat as implementation moves forward. Therefore, a client should remain flexible and willing to learn the culture and motivations of a new team. In some cases, however, clients are angry because the willing and agreeable team they met when they were seeking a provider is gone and they have to work with a new group. They may resist the suggestions of the new group and wittingly, or unwittingly, damage the outsourcing initiative.

Another reason for failure in the early stages of an outsourcing initiative is the client's mistaken belief, that once they have selected an outsourcing provider, they do not have to be involved. In actuality, the most critical period for any outsourcing relationship is the first 90 days after an agreement is signed. In other words, outsourcing is not a "hands-off" process.

In many cases, transition from selection to the first three months after startup is underestimated, taken for granted, and not given enough effort.

You and your provider must work hard to prevent this from happening. Understand and accept the fact that you are dealing with new people and a new culture and be prepared to make adjustments. Teams should be built to foster communication and knowledge transfer.

This transition and acceptance period is not easy, and it takes commitment and resourcefulness on the part of all involved to make it a success. This chapter discusses the transition from engagement to implementation, selecting the relationship manager, teaming for a strong transition, roles and responsibilities, communication, and additional tips for putting the outsourcing relationship in motion.

START-UP: THE TRANSITION TO A WORKING RELATIONSHIP

The working relationship between a company and its outsourcing provider is defined early in the process. It is somewhat defined in the RFP specifications and in the provider's responses, and then it is strengthened as the company acquires knowledge of their provider's corporate characteristics and checks their references.

The relationship is further developed during the period of contracting and negotiations. At this time, a company and provider define scope, responsibilities, and service expectations that will serve as the outsourcing "rule book" once engagement is complete. This is often when companies make the mistake of thinking that their work with the provider is over. Nothing could be further from the truth. The real work begins once the contract is signed; the actions leading up to that time are just a prelude.

The transition from contract to working relationship must be a team effort. Your company cannot afford to be passive during start-up (usually 90 days, but in more complex relationships, it can last as long as a year). Become involved in all aspects of the outsourcing initiative, communicating your needs and acquiring information and input from the outsourcing provider. You should include the provider in planning meetings to discuss strategy and performance. The provider should, in turn, be responsive to any pertinent changes and communicate any problems or issues encountered as you both move forward.

During this time, you and your chosen provider must also be aware of and avoid the following major outsourcing relationship pitfalls:

- Unrealistic goals. The first 90 (or more) days after start-up are not going to be perfect. Your provider is going to struggle to hit the metric targets during that period as they make the adjustments to work with your company. Setting goals that include going live at full production speed or efficiency with no mistakes is unrealistic and may damage your relationship with the provider.

- False perceptions. All providers and customers make mistakes along the way. Encourage your outsourcing provider to be candid and honest early in the relationship about mistakes rather than accepting their sales team's assurances that "all will be well." Not only will this end any false perceptions, but the provider will present you with invaluable information about the lessons they have learned.

- Lowered expectations. Client-provider relationships are labeled as failures when one party does not do what the other expects. The key to preventing this is to manage expectations. The learning curve requires time to get things right, so be patient and pace the start-up expectations to realistic levels.

Below are some of the other common mistakes that companies and outsourcing providers can make during the transition period.

Providers

Not having executive support • Relying on "boilerplate" information for all pricing • Making last-minute decisions • Failing to finalize the term sheet or contract • Not dedicating the integration teams to a sole project • Missing specific regional Human Resource issues, such as employee quality and quantity • Stopping communication with the client • Sending implementation team home before the working relationship is in a steady state • Not developing start up/steady state metrics with client • Not measuring performance during startup • Not communicating metrics to employees • Letting problems move forward without resolution • Not being proactive with communication, forcing client to initiate • Failing to adjust processes and retrain to address problem areas and quality issues

Clients

Poor decision-making mechanisms • Getting too comfortable with the provider at the expense of others • Not reading/understanding the service agreements and metrics clearly • Making last minute requests or setting new expectations • Failing to finalize the contract • Shortening the lead time or moving up the start date • Maintaining a hands-off attitude, not offering to help • Poor or no internal employee communication • Not accepting any responsibility in the outsourcing relationship • Internal team (expertise) not being committed to full implementation • Expecting 100% from the Provider on Day 1 of the contract • Using metrics as a "whip" instead of a tool for managing the relationship • Reacting severely to first quality breakdown • Trying to remove itself as the information source for the project

Implementation pitfalls

The end results of these pitfalls are non-performance, cost increases, and failure to achieve continuous improvement.

An excellent way to avoid these pitfalls is to manage expectations early in the relationship, because unrealistic expectations create a shaky foundation for any initiative. You and your selected provider should have already developed metrics during the contracting period (as described in Chapter 9). One recommended method for managing expectations is to go through the contract and ensure that each requirement is being met. Then, review your transition plan and be sure that each step has been addressed. In other words, work the plan, and do not let time pressures or surprises create a false sense of urgency or even panic. We also suggest that you and your provider conduct roundtables with senior management to address issues and concerns.

On several occasions, Tompkins Associates has been involved in the audit of an existing relationship and has acted as an expert witness in a failed relationship. In the majority of these cases where performance was considered poor, one or several of the above conditions were not met. Therefore, proper management of the relationship is very important to ensure that the other conditions are met.

SELECTING THE RELATIONSHIP MANAGER

Both parties should also address the issue of project relationship management at this time. It is possible for each organization to have a project manager, although some outsourcers prefer to have one project manager, usually from the provider's organization. This is often a good tactic. Many of the more capable providers have been through a number of start-ups, and their project managers bring a great deal of expertise to the table. They understand the teaming concept and can provide valuable insights, identify organizational issues, and communicate proactively.

The project manager's responsibilities are:

- Reporting individual team progress to the steering committee;
- Maintaining the overall timeline;
- Maintaining the transition budget;
- Ensuring that each team is aligned and meeting with their objectives; and
- Facilitating the team's progress.

Outsourcing Start-up Controversy: Providers Are at Fault

It's no secret that the success of an outsourcing initiative hinges on implementation and perform-ance. When an outsourcing initiative fails or struggles because of poor implementation and per-formance issues early in the relationship, the typical verdict is that the provider is at fault. In fact, poor startup and an inability to execute in the early stages of an initiative continue to be the largest criticisms leveled against providers.

Companies that have been through failed start ups will tell you that the provider:

- Underestimated the resources required;
- Oversold and under-performed;
- Did not truly understand their business;
- Was unable to react quickly to problems; and
- Did not communicate.

Is this truly the reason for the failures? Often, if you dig a little deeper, you will discover that the client was laboring under the false impression that because they handed over the "keys to the kingdom," they no longer had a key role in the initiative. As a result, the following happened:

- There was no full disclosure of expectations;
- Communication and information flow was poor;
- Unrealistic timelines were set;
- Client failed to commit resources or expertise;
- Client takes the mindset that the vendor is the expert. As far as logistics and management of operations are concerned, this is true. However, what they are not is an expert on the client's business, which can negate any of the provider's expertise;

Too often, the providers are "doomed to failure before they even begin". A successful out-sourcing initiative is a shared effort, requiring resources and commitment from both parties. If the actions below have been done, there is no reason the start-up should fail:

- The outsourcing selection process has been conducted properly;
- Due diligence has been performed;
- Detailed plans have been developed;
- The correct resources have been dedicated; and
- Expectations have been clearly defined throughout the process.

Successful start-ups always have a common underlying theme: effort and contribution from both parties.

Who manages the relationship is another question that needs to be answered by the outsourcer and the provider. Management selection should not be handled by one party, although, ultimately, the out-sourcer will have the final say. Therefore, everyone involved should be aware that the best relationship managers:

- Understand change;
- Have excellent communications skills;

- Are strong at building relationships;
- Are strong at maintaining relationships;
- Have a desire to manage, not to actually do; and
- Can create an environment where successes are celebrated.

The ideal relationship manager is not necessarily a strong, technically-skilled individual with a strong background in the function being outsourced, such as manufacturing. Instead, the managers of outsourcing relationships must be team-oriented problem solvers. They must be able to address performance issues and results and discuss corrective action and the need for continuous improvement.

Relationship managers must be people who will not tell the provider how to run the operation. They must resist saying, "That is not how we have always done that." They remain aware of the fact that they have outsourced a function and, therefore, the job at hand is no longer how to perform the operation. Instead, it is about how to meet requirements and service levels.

> **The Relationship Manager – One Client's Perspective**
> Tompkins Associates was hired by a client, and together we selected a warehouse/transportation provider and were in the initial steps of moving the relationship forward. As we discussed finding the right individual to manage this very large outsourcing relationship, the client said, "You know, when I really sit back and think this through, I'm not looking for a relationship manager that understands how to lay-out a warehouse or the best means of cubing out an outbound truck. What I am really seeking is an individual who understands how to manage and measure relationships. That's what will make us successful." Truer words have never been spoken. This is how third-party relationships must be managed if they are going to be successful, and it starts from the point of moving forward.

Teaming for a Strong Relationship

Essentially, there are two groups involved in the start-up process. The first group consists of people from your company, along with the provider, who understand implementation and project management and its transient role in the relationship. The second group is comprised of the people who will be responsible for the day-to-day business of the initiative and its processes. Each of these groups should play an important role during start-up, and any teams built for the effort should include representatives from each group.

The start-up teams created by each organization should also mirror each other. Therefore, your company and your provider need to form teams for the following start-up functions:

- Steering committee;
- Technology (WMS, OM, CMS, etc.);
- Risk management;
- Product transition;
- Human Resources;
- Process documentation; and
- Training.

These teams must work with the relationship manager to control the implementation of the partnership and develop the path for ongoing management of the partnership. It is best when all the teams work as a small company with the sole purpose of a successful implementation. The amount of time required by the teams varies based on the phase of the implementation. Some of the teams such as risk management and training might have heavier commitments initially but taper off after the initial start-up weeks. Other teams that are more operations-focused are full-time positions.

The individuals that make up these teams must be project focused. They should not be the people who will ultimately run the operations. Their scope is to support the operators and take some of the firefighting and process development and implementation away from them.

Together, you and your outsourcing provider should also establish a steering committee made up of senior management from both parties. This committee can be used by the relationship manager to help provide focus and problem resolution. The relationship manager will work with the teams to determine what, if anything, will be brought to the steering committee meetings. The steering committee meetings should be frequent enough to support the implementation teams but not so much as to take away the decision-making ability of the relationship manager and his teams.

The main objectives of the steering committee are to:

- Clear the path of obstacles for the teams;
- Provide required resources; and
- Serve as a problem escalation mechanism.

While teams are being formed, it is important to define the roles and responsibilities of all involved and establish rules of engagement. The next section discusses this issue.

ROLES AND RESPONSIBILITIES

Both sides own an equal share in contributing to a successful start-up. A major aspect of this is creating and understanding responsibilities and ground rules. This is the time to develop rules of engagement — a step that is often missed once an agreement between outsourcer and provider is reached.

Establishing rules of engagement during the implementation will facilitate the relationship. Some of the questions to consider are:

- How often do we meet? At first, meetings should be frequent, perhaps once or twice a week, depending on the size of the outsourcing initiative, until everyone is comfortable with the transition and each other. However, after the teams have been working together for a number of months, the meetings can become less frequent;
- Who in each organization will be involved in the start-up and transition? The answer to this question is derived from the teams that each organization has created internally for the project. It is critical that all parties make one another aware of these teams and who is on them. Also important is that communication between parties continues if teams re-form or team members change during the initiative start-up;
- How will we treat each other? This question may seem odd at first because the answer should be obvious. However, it is not. Each company involved in an outsourcing initiative has a different approach to doing business. Some companies prefer a more formal relationship with a well-defined chain of command. They prefer to operate through documentation and approvals. Other companies are more informal and prefer to make decisions in meetings and gain consensus verbally before proceeding. Of course, no matter what decision is made, it is important for everyone involved to make respect and decent behavior a priority;
- What are the absolute "Nos?" This is an important question to address. Both the outsourcer and the provider might want to avoid establishing boundaries and discussing drawbacks before

start-up for fear of appearing negative or demanding. However, outsourcers must tell the provider they have chosen what they absolutely will not accept and vice versa; otherwise, your initiative may go down a path you do not want. In other words, if neither you nor your provider sets limits about what is acceptable in the venture and what is not, there may be unwanted surprises down the road;

- What is the problem escalation chain? Problem escalation is important because it is what will keep the transition and relationship moving forward. Problem escalation is addressed in the contract; however, it should be revisited during start-up. Each party should establish a problem escalation system or hierarchy for defining and prioritizing problems and bringing them to the attention of the correct level within their organization so that they might be resolved with expedience.

Answering these questions will allow you and your provider to establish the rules of engagement, as well as the roles and responsibilities of both parties. This significantly reduces the chance that you will encounter problems that often occur when there are no ground rules put in place early on. If your provider is aware of what you absolutely will not accept, for example, then neither of you runs the risk of putting a policy or process in place that is contrary to how you do business.

COMMUNICATION PLAN AND EXECUTION

Most outsourcing relationships begin with the best intentions, they often encounter pitfalls in the early stages. Communication — or the lack of it — is a significant pitfall. Another pitfall is the FUD factor: fear, uncertainty, and doubt. People are afraid of the unknown, and it is human nature to resist change. Throughout transition and start-up, there will be people who complain and do not like the "new" way of doing things.

The best way to address these possible pitfalls is to spend as much time as you can gathering information. Then, you should flood the provider and your own employees with information. However, you must do this in an orderly fashion with a solid communications plan that focuses on the quality of information shared.

The first step in developing a communication plan is to set clear communication expectations up-front. Decide early, while you are defining roles and responsibilities, who is going to communicate what to whom and when. Then, as you would with any other part of the project roll-out, document those communications requirements in the form of a plan and publish it.

While you and your provider are creating the communication plan, you should make sure that it has the following characteristics:

- It addresses the "5 Ws" (who, what, when, where, and why);
- Its foundation is constant, honest, and open communications;
- It assures the accuracy of data and information at go-live;
- It provides everyone involved in the outsourcing initiative with the information needed to do their jobs;
- It ensures that all concerns are heard and addressed;
- It defines the process for the creation of the first reports, service levels and invoices, as well as a method for agreement on the first edition of each of these documents;
- It provides the means for ending complaint cycles with positive feedback and communications; and
- It makes provisions for celebrating a successful go-live.

An unusual but successful method for making sure that the communications plan is followed and that both outsourcer and provider are communicating thoroughly is to locate the relationship manager at the provider's corporate headquarters. Consider the client we mentioned earlier in a sidebar. When we got to the point of hiring the relationship manager, the client's next revelation was a simple statement: "You know, it's not the provider's warehouse operation where our relationship manager should be residing. It's the provider's head office."

We were impressed. This client truly understood that, if they were really going to get this very important relationship started and moving forward, they had to focus on communication. They did not simply pay lip service to this notion; they wanted constant, honest, and open communications to the point of putting their relationship management in the area where the important decisions were discussed and made. This concept of putting a relationship manager in the provider's corporate location may not be for everyone. However, the point of the story is that this client realized that battles may be won in the trenches, but the best battle plans are communicated from headquarters.

> **Communication: The 3PL Perspective**
>
> "Those of us who are good at logistics, at the business of moving stuff around, are not necessarily the best relationship managers," says Bill Gates, CEO of Standard Logistics in Columbia, SC, a subsidiary of UTi Worldwide Inc. Standard works hard to overcome that tendency by posting several relationship managers to a given account, each of whom concentrates on a different level of the business.
>
> "In our business, relationships are critical, and when a person leaves a company, your business is at risk," Gates says. "It just makes good business sense and it does facilitate communications to stay networked at different levels of the organization."
>
> Gates says his successful logistics ventures have occurred when the clients who hired Standard had a reputation for working with their logistics provider to solve the issues that come up — clients who are really looking to create a partnership. "We're all going to have bumps in the road, we're all going to have problems, [but] they've learned how to solve those and work through those and get to the root cause and collaborate," he says.[1]

MORE TIPS FOR PUTTING THE RELATIONSHIP IN MOTION

To be successful during the start-up period, both parties must focus on meeting the following key requirements:

- Have senior management buy-in and commitment. It is important that everyone close to the project, but particularly senior management, understand the scope, goals and timeline of the process.
- Be brutally honest. Agree to be open, no matter how difficult the news. Information about the outsourcing relationship must be broadly, consistently, and openly presented to a cross-section of people within both the company and the provider. Do not try to hide problems or gloss them over. This will only damage the relationship and possibly the transition. Being open about difficult issues will help you and the provider identify the root causes behind these problems and solve them.
- Create a joint sign-off process and have key elements go through that process. Establishing a regular, ongoing process for business planning, evolution, and communications is critical to keep the relationship evolving. Decisions must be made with respect to the level of and frequency of formal and informal communications and meetings.
- Celebrate small successes along the way. This will keep everyone motivated to participate in improving the performance of the outsource relationship.

- Do not keep the initiative a secret. Instead, let all involved know. If appropriate, consider holding a launch party.
- Solve problems as they arise. A common mistake during start-up is to avoid mentioning problems in hopes they will just disappear. Problems usually do not disappear; instead, they can escalate. As soon as you or your provider encounter a problem, you should work together to identify its root causes and solutions.
- Create a timeline and stick to it. This timeline should include more than simply the implementation start and end dates. Instead, it should include milestones and accomplishments from the selection of the provider until the contract end date.

If you work to make your start-up and early relationship with the provider meet these requirements, function together as a team, have a good communications plan in place, and ensure everyone is clear about the rules of engagement and their roles and responsibilities, then the period from provider selection to start-up will be successful.

---

1 Bennett Voyles, "Dear Miss Lonelycarts." *Operations and Fulfillment,* May 1, 2004. http://opsandfulfillment.com/mag/fulfillment_dear_miss_lonelycarts/

ON THE ELEVATOR

The period of transition from selection through implementation is underestimated, taken for granted, and not given enough effort. Work hard to prevent this from happening. Both parties must be able to understand and accept the fact that you are dealing with new people and a new culture and be prepared to make adjustments.

During this time, you and your chosen outsourcing provider must also be aware of and avoid the following major outsourcing relationship pitfalls:

- Unrealistic goals;
- False perceptions; and
- Lowered expectations.

The negative results of these pitfalls are non-performance, cost increases, and failure to achieve continuous improvement. To prevent these difficulties, you should define and manage expectations, develop metrics, conduct roundtables with senior management, and review your transition plan often.

Another important consideration: who will manage the relationship?

The relationship manager should be chosen by both parties. Technical ability is not as important as the ability to lead, make difficult decisions, and manage others.

During the transition period from selection to start-up, teams should be built to foster communication and knowledge transition. These teams should consist of members from your company and the provider's. Both you and the provider should also make sure that any teams you create within your organizations mirror one another, and you should

decide whether each of you should have a project manager or if one project manager from the provider's company will suffice.

Establishing rules of engagement will facilitate the relationship. Some of the questions to consider are: how often to meet, who will be involved in start-up and transition, how each party will treat the other, what is strictly forbidden, and what hierarchy will be used for problem escalation? Answering these questions will allow you and your provider to establish the rules of engagement, as well as the roles and responsibilities of your company and theirs.

Develop a solid communications plan that focuses on the quality of information shared. The first step is to set clear communication expectations up-front. Decide early on who is going to communicate what to whom and when. Then, as you would with any other part of the project roll-out, document those communications requirements in the form of a plan and publish it.

Other guidelines for a successful start up are:

- Gain senior management buy-in and commitment;
- Agree to be open;
- Create a joint sign-off process;
- Celebrate small successes along the way;
- Do not keep the initiative a secret;
- Solve problems as they arise; and
- Create a timeline and stick to it.

Establishing the Ongoing Relationship

INTRODUCTION

A successful start-up indicates that an outsourcing initiative is on the right path, but it is a long way from ultimate success. To prevent failure down the road, take the relationship you have just formed with your outsourcing provider during the period between selection and start-up and build upon it. Investing the time and resources to make the outsourcing relationship work after start-up is vital if you want the initiative to succeed and flourish.

An outsourcing relationship, like any relationship, has a life cycle (Figure 1).

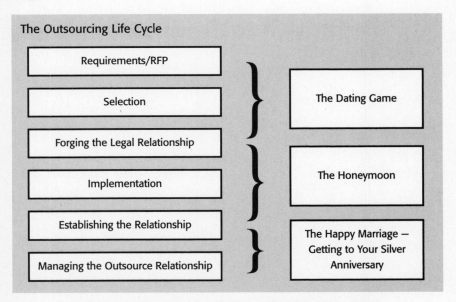

Figure 1: The Outsourcing Relationship Life Cycle

Throughout this book, we have explored the early stages of the out-sourcing relationship lifecycle—from sending out an RFI to creating the relationship during start-up. Now it's time to look at the outsourcing relationship life cycle in order to learn how to build a lasting relationship and establish a continuous improvement process, recognize signs that the relationship is struggling, and understand how to overcome difficulties.

THE OUTSOURCING RELATIONSHIP LIFE CYCLE

Outsourcing relationships are between both organizations and people. Therefore, several types of relationships can form during and after implementation. The two most common are vendor/client and partnership. Ideally, your post-implementation relationship should move beyond vendor/client and toward partnership. Yes, there is a contract between your company and the provider. But more importantly, there is a relationship between the people in your company and the people in the provider's organization. Adequately investing in the people side will cement that relationship.

In many respects, as shown in Figure 1, the relationship between a company and an outsourcing provider is like the process of getting married. There is a courtship period that starts out with dating (requirements and RFP process), followed by the wedding and honeymoon (selection, start-up, and the first months after start-up), and then, finally, a happy marriage (maintaining and managing the outsourcing relationship). During the courtship period, a company and outsourcing provider get to know each other and discover that each likes what the other has to offer. They both decide to take the relationship to the next level, and a proposal is made. Once the proposal is accepted, the legal process of getting married occurs (as in contract negotiations). After this process is completed, there is a big wedding with a great deal of fanfare followed by the honeymoon.

But truly, an outsourcing relationship and a marriage resemble each other most after the wedding, which is comparable to a successful implementation. During this time, it seems as if everyone is going to live happily ever after because the wedding and the honeymoon have been so successful. However, neither of these events can ensure that the out-sourcing initiative, or marriage, will be long lasting. In both types of relationships, you must work to build upon the early successes.

BUILDING A LASTING RELATIONSHIP

The key to building upon the early successes of the relationship is maintaining the atmosphere of teamwork and open communications that you established during the selection and start-up processes. Otherwise, the relationship with your outsourcing provider will suffer. During the selection process, both the company and the outsourcing provider do everything in their power to sell themselves. The provider has offered glowing references from other clients and reassurance that they can handle your business. You have, in turn, told the provider that the transition of functions from your house to theirs will be smooth and that everyone is on board. At the time of these assertions, you believe them to be true. But as previously mentioned, once the ink is dry on the contract, things start to change. The salespeople move out of the picture, and the people who will get the job done step up. If neither party is prepared for this shift, it will be difficult to survive past the "courtship."

The same phenomenon happens after implementation. Many times, the personalities change again as your company shifts its focus to primary core competencies and your provider is now fully handling the functions that were outsourced. By recognizing that an outsourcing relationship is constantly shifting, changing, and re-forming with a number of different players, you can be ready for the shift in personalities that come after implementation, just as you were ready for the shift following selection.

As you begin building a lasting relationship with your provider, remember that there is no "off the shelf" approach. Establishing a relationship geared toward long-term success is as much an art as it is a science. The first step is to give the outsourcer the same acceptance that you would any new members of your organization. Avoid any hint of an "us versus them" mentality because that encourages poor communication and unnecessary hostility. At the same time, recognize that you and your provider will disagree and that such disagreements are healthy. The trick is communicating properly so that the disagreements become an impetus for moving the relationship and initiative forward.

Once you have adopted an acceptance mindset and agreed to communicate openly and honestly with the provider, you can build that lasting relationship necessary for outsourcing success. This process includes:

- Establishing a regular, ongoing process for business planning, evolution and communications. This is critical if you want to keep the relationship evolving. You and your outsourcing provider must decide the levels and frequency of formal and informal communications and meetings.

- Implementing a rewards structure of gain sharing or goal sharing. As noted in Chapter 9, building a reward structure into the relationship with your provider will create a win-win scenario because both sides are motivated to participate in improving the performance of the outsourcing relationship.

- Ensuring that there are regular, ongoing executive interactions. Depending upon the magnitude of the relationship, this may require a regular executive-to-executive, face-to-face interaction. There are outsourcing relationships that do not promote high-level communications and teamwork after the transition period is over. Those involved mistakenly believe that only the people doing the work and managing the project need to communicate after start-up. Executive communication is critical to the success of any outsourcing relationship. Otherwise, small disagreements can grow into huge problems. Structured status reporting activities and unstructured, informal communications about the evolution of the relationship should be part of the interaction process.

- Reviewing the RFP and the contract after implementation and identifying surprises, changes, and problem areas. Any areas in which reality differs from expectations should be discussed as soon as possible. These discussions will identify opportunities for improvement.

- Measuring performance against the initial goals established for outsourcing. This needs to be much more than a cost vs. budget analysis — it calls for a full, robust analysis of the implementation and the outsourcing initiative.

- Conducting two types of formal "lessons learned" roundtable meetings. One type is a meeting that your company holds alone on the topic of outsourcing. The second type of meeting is between your company and the provider, with a focus on your relationship.

- Encouraging creativity and innovation on both sides of the relationship. There are certain processes and rules that must be followed in an outsourcing relationship. However, as you progress past implementation, remain flexible and open to new ideas and solutions to challenges that will develop along the way.

As with any initiative, a key component of building a lasting outsourcing relationship is emphasis on continuous improvement.

CONTINUOUS IMPROVEMENT AND THE OUTSOURCING RELATIONSHIP

To practice continuous improvement, you and your outsourcing provider need to understand collaboration, cooperation, and true partnership. Although companies involved in an outsourcing relationship may pay lip service to partnership, true partnering is rarely practiced.

To create the right kind of partnership with your outsourcing provider, all organizational units within each company should be 100% directed towards the success of the initiative. There can be no adversarial relationships between the outsourcer and provider. Instead, both groups must function as a cohesive, collective whole. The goal is to eliminate the "we vs. they" problem that can undermine such relationships.

To accomplish this goal, make sure you and the provider have:

- The characteristics of a successful relationship;
- Cooperation and collaboration;
- A plan for long-term success;
- A true partnership; and
- A Continuous Improvement Success Path Forward.

The sections that follow discuss these steps in detail.

The Characteristics of a Successful Relationship

Everyone involved in the initiative must understand the following characteristics of a successful outsourcing relationship:

- Shared vision — Hold a consistent vision of where the initiative is headed.
- Shared values — Adhere to a level of business ethics and honesty beyond levels traditionally viewed as the norm.
- Shared expectations — Have well-defined and understood expectations that are shared by all team players and serve as a basis for teamwork.
- Shared commitment — Be committed to the initiative's long-term success.
- Shared confidence — Maintain complete confidence in one another.

- Shared responsibility — Share responsibility for success and failure. All players must be accountable for their efforts and the initiative.

Cooperation and Collaboration

Having meetings and writing memos does not create cooperation in an outsourcing initiative. Joint participation creates cooperation. After start-up, the team must operate as a unit. By cooperating, confidence and commitment to the success of the initiative grows and a sense of excellence emerges. Conflict is viewed as an opportunity to learn. There is no win/lose mentality, but rather an attitude of mutual discovery and support of the team's growth.

The real type of cooperation necessary for a successful, strong outsourcing relationship is actually more than cooperation. It is collaboration, which creates the synergy to drive a robust relationship. To begin the process of collaboration, ask these questions:

- What can we do to foster a collaborative culture?
- How can we overcome individualism?
- How can we communicate our belief in collaboration?
- How can we begin the revolution toward collaboration right now?
- How will we celebrate our success?

A Plan for Long-Term Success

After selection, the companies involved in an outsourcing initiative develop a plan for start-up and implementation. But what many companies fail to do is develop a plan for long-term success, and even fewer develop a plan for building on that success. This is a mistake. You and your outsourcing provider must have a plan to guarantee that the gains made during start-up are not lost. Therefore, when you plan for start-up, look beyond this phase and make sure the elements are in place for the initiative to be successful six months, one year, two years, and even five years down the road.

One key element involves handling the large cultural or business process changes that occur after the partnership has stabilized. Because this is still a business relationship, there will be an end to a contract. There will be some portions of the relationship that will change during the contract life; this is normal. Distinguishing the changes that can take place under the current agreement, along with those that are best held off until the contract re-negotiation period, is a process in which both parties need to work together.

If there are ideas and changes in business that are best dealt with at the end of the contract life, and if your timeframe dictates it and the relationship is solid, it is best to start working on these initiatives prior to the renegotiation period. In this way, each party has a good understanding of what will be expected of them.

In a case where changes are occurring as a natural part of the relationship, both parties must stay on top of them together. Changes such as these should follow a process of:

- Communication of the desired changes;
- Evaluation of operational, systems, service, equipment, and personnel requirements;
- Assessment of the risk of implementation;
- Joint justification of the proposed changes and the effects on fees based on the current contract;
- Development of a joint implementation plan;
- Implementation; and
- Follow-up assessment of success.

Don't forget to consider ways to build on the initiative's long-term success. Work toward a win/win evolution of the relationship whereby your company holds on to the gains made during each initiative milestone and never rests on its laurels. As you continually look for new ways to succeed, increase commitment, dedication, and cooperation.

True Partnership

In an outsourcing initiative, true partnerships are long-term collaborative relationships between an outsourcer and a provider that are based on trust and a mutual desire to work together for the benefit of the other and the initiative. The characteristics of a true partnership are:

- Commitment to long-term relationships based on trust and a true understanding of the partner's business;
- Belief in sharing information, planning, scheduling, risks, rewards, problems, solutions, and opportunities;
- Commitment to working together toward improvements in quality, product, accuracy, and management;
- Resolution and agreement to build on each other's strengths, increase business, and invest in the long-term partnership;

- Commitment to systems integration and organizational interdependence while still retaining individual identities to ensure innovation and creativity;
- Consensus that frequent commitment at all levels of the organization must occur and that partnership proximity is important and will be mutually addressed;
- Commitment to the flexibility required to ensure the best overall performance of the partnership.

True Partnerships with 3PLs: Air Products & Chemicals Inc.

Air Products & Chemicals Inc., the world's only combined gases and chemicals company, has been outsourcing its warehousing operations for more than 20 years, reports Patti Platia. As supervisor of off-site management and field support for the Pennsylvania company, she works with 13 third-party logistics providers in North America.

For example, Platia has worked closely with Faure Brothers for years, storing material at its Calumet, Ill., warehouse. The 3PL performs the typical receiving and shipping, relabeling, and transporting of international containers. In addition, Faure Brothers distributes products from a facility that Air Products jointly owns in the area.

Platia has developed a list of attributes that she looks for in a third-party logistics provider. These attributes include:

- The ability to handle all aspects of Air Products' business, including hazmat storage facilities;
- Regulatory compliance based on commodities stored;
- Financial stability;
- Honest and open communications; no "smoke and mirrors";
- Very high service levels; and
- A rigorous quality process.

Platia is demanding of the 3PLs, but also supportive. She treats them as integral members of the Air Products' team. "I work closely between our customer service organization and our warehouses. If issues arise, I investigate the specifics of the situation, see how the provider contributes, and determine whether our instructions could have led to the situation," Platia says. "Together we decide what we can do to prevent recurrence."

The warehouses and Air Products are in constant contact, and they work together to head off potential problems. For example, a 3PL and Air Products are each aware when either party has a new customer service representative (CSR) on board. They watch carefully to ensure that no problems crop up that a more experienced CSR might catch, and then let their partner know if the new CSR needs additional training.

Air Products finds the right balance in providing oversight. For example, the company provides warehouses with an operations manual, giving explicit instructions on expected outcomes. "We let them decide the best way to get to the outcome unless there are areas where we've had problems, then we give specific instructions," Platia says. "The warehouses have the opportunity to review the manual and come to us if they have any questions or would like us to consider a better practice. It's all about working together to meet requirements."[1]

Forming a true partnership requires discarding the traditional relationships common between organizations today. The objective of creating true partnerships is to generate the same synergy between organizations that the collaboration process creates within one organization. This means understanding that the term relationship is not synonymous with partnership; instead, a relationship must be transformed into a partnership.

As you work toward forming a true partnership, keep the following information in mind:

- No two relationships develop the same way;
- Relationships evolve as comfortable bonds between individuals;
- A positive chemistry must exist between two parties to create a relationship — not only during the sales cycle, but more importantly at the operational level;
- Partnerships evolve from understanding hopes and dreams and anticipating a bright future;
- Each party must know itself and understand what it is seeking from the partnership;
- Acceptance by indirectly involved parties, such as stockholders and the government, is as important to the perpetuation of the partnership as acceptance by directly affected parties;
- The relationship, at its core, has interest in the well-being of the other parties along with the well-being of the partnership;
- Expectations of how the relationship will develop must be articulated; and
- Compatibility is key to a long-term relationship.

The goal of a true partnership in an outsourcing initiative is to blur identities so that you can focus on the initiative rather than on individual companies. Not making distinctions between companies allows improvement and growth in your partnership and ensures outsourcing success.

The Continuous Improvement Success Path Forward

The Continuous Improvement Success Path Forward is the methodology for establishing continuous improvement once the collaboration and cooperation between the outsourcer and the provider have been set. The path forward has the following steps:

- Establish continuous improvement teams. These teams drive the continuous improvement process. They must be cross functional in nature, and their members should have demonstrated in the past that they are capable of achieving continuous improvements, breakthroughs, and innovation to enhance performance. Frequent meetings are necessary to develop specific recommendations and action plans in order to achieve peak performance in all areas.

- Conduct roundtables regularly throughout the lifetime of the initiative. A roundtable is a meeting of peers for discussion and the exchange of views. Outsourcing roundtables should have representatives from all companies and functions involved in the initiative. They provide a facilitated, interactive opportunity for suppliers and customers to share ideas about products and markets, question existing beliefs, and uncover new opinions. The information collected from these roundtables provides unique input into the development of a strategic plan for continuous improvement, and the relationships they foster are invaluable. Participants are more clearly exposed to the complexity of outsourcing relationships and can become more confident as together they develop solutions from the roundtable process.

- Define continuous improvement vision and evidence of success. A continuous improvement vision is a clear description of where the initiative is headed. It should be stated so that the present is described as a past condition of the future, not as a future condition of the past. Milestones are the evidence of success signaling that you are on the right track.

- Define prioritized areas for improvement. A benchmark assessment is a very useful tool in defining opportunities for continuous improvement. The organization then focuses its continuous improvement efforts on the areas identified as weaknesses in the assessment.

- Implement continuous improvement team recommendations. The team's recommendations should be shared with the outsourcing initiative team for review and approval. Once suggestions are approved, they should be implemented. The steering team must communicate the approved recommendations and remain committed to them throughout the implementation process.

- Assess evidence of success. Those involved with the implementation of the continuous improvement team's recommendations should maintain an ongoing record that tracks performance against the defined evidence of success. The record should also be periodically reviewed to prioritize the next opportunities for improvement.

- Define new prioritized opportunities for improvement. After the evidence of success records show that performance has improved, the outsourcing initiative team can begin to prioritize opportunities for the next iteration of the continuous improvement process. This is truly continuous improvement in action! Your company and your provider should never stop looking for ways to improve. Once you have a continuous improvement process in place, your outsourcing relationship has a greater chance of growing, improving, and remaining strong. However, you can improve these chances even more by learning to recognize the signs that your relationship may be in trouble. The next section discusses these warning signs.

Continuous Improvement and Communication Create Award-Winning Outsourcing

Recently, the outsourcing relationship of SAIC and Entergy Services, Inc. was acknowledged as one of the world's best. SAIC and Entergy were awarded a 2004 Outsourcing Excellence Award (sponsored by the Everest Group, Forbes, and Wharton Executive Education) as one of the world's seven most outstanding outsourcing relationships. The SAIC and Entergy relationship was named Best Refreshed, acknowledging the success of the parties in keeping their long-standing relationship responsive to changing goals and enhancing value outcomes. The ongoing commitment to continuous improvement and performance management throughout Entergy's organization also made Entergy the winner of the 2004 Gartner Technology, Organization and Process (TOP) Performance Award, and SAIC's role was acknowledged in the win.

In 1999, Entergy, one of the largest U.S. utilities, selected SAIC to provide Entergy with comprehensive IT outsourcing services. The five-year agreement was an open book contract, using a shared risk/award model and quality-based performance incentive. It also included a unique feature: employees were given the choice of having Entergy or SAIC as their employer. As a result, SAIC transitioned 350 former Entergy employees and 100 contractors.

SAIC assumed responsibility for operations and support of a wide array of Entergy's traditional IT services functions. These functions included data center operations for the corporate center, operations of a new Integrated Services Management Center, operations and support of distributed servers, desktop support, telecommunications and field services, and applications development, support, and maintenance.

In 2001 and 2002, modifications were made to the contract to help deliver new, transformational objectives and meet anticipated cost challenges for Entergy. Today, SAIC supports all business units across Entergy, providing expertise in different technology areas. These additional areas of support include enterprise applications integration, PeopleSoft® consulting, e-business enablement and architecture, software engineering process improvement, integrated services management, security and penetration testing, technology consulting, and nuclear plant support.

According to Entergy CIO Ray Johnson, "The relationship works for two key reasons: (1) We have both committed ourselves to a set of contractual governance/relationship management practices and principles for which we are both incentivized; and (2) the individuals who lead the relationship on both sides are personally committed to openness, honesty and continuous improvement."

Commitment, openness, honesty, and continuous improvement: good advice for any relationship — and a great formula for a winning outsourcing alliance.[2]

TROUBLE IN PARADISE: SIGNS OF A STRUGGLING OUTSOURCING RELATIONSHIP

The outsourcing relationship after start-up is not a continuation of the "honeymoon." The good communication, understanding, and trust that resulted in a successful start-up and that, presumably, started during selection can be lost without effort. Promises made by sales personnel can come back to haunt you and your provider if they are not addressed. Communications can break down, and the result can be that neither you nor your provider has any idea of what drives the other. In the end, you may look at one another and say, "I can't believe we ever entered into this relationship."

A key objective going into the relationship was to produce a win/win situation. Now it is time to sit down and review how this has evolved. The fact is if both parties are not happy with the relationship, neither party will be happy with the relationship. If you are not careful, "divorce" will be the final outcome. This can occur in the form of:

- Bringing the functions back in-house;
- Extending the contract at added expense; or
- Taking the contract out to bid.

These are all expensive, unnecessary outcomes to a relationship that had such promise. To prevent these negative results, communicate constantly and learn to recognize the signs that your relationship is in trouble. For the outsourcer, behaviors that can lead to a failed initiative include:

- Poor executive communication. Understanding each other's business goals is very important. Not understanding your provider's goals can cause the relationship to fail.
- The elimination of daily interactions between managers of both parties. This is the death throe of a relationship. It can spiral into differences in perception on issues and costs.
- Failing to maintain metrics and monitor the relationship. Well-maintained metrics are the basis for continuous improvement and promote conversation on issues.
- Not accepting responsibility. As the client, you may have outsourced this operation, but you still have responsibility for your supply chain. If a customer complains about service, it is still your problem.

- Using metrics as a whip and not a tool. When metrics become the stick with which to beat the provider, two problems arise. One is that most likely the outsourced process suffers, and the second is that an unhealthy win-lose attitude develops.

For the outsourcing provider, the following behaviors can lead to trouble:

- Poor executive communication. This will have the same effects on the provider as the client.
- Failure to be proactive. The provider must be proactive and inform the client that they have been so. Failing at either of these two will indicate to the client that the provider does not care.
- Not measuring and reporting performance. Measuring performance for a client is the best way for a provider to show its strengths and communicate issues or weaknesses in the current process. This is also a two-way street: a provider must be willing to tell a client when they are not performing to the metrics they must achieve.
- Not developing metrics with the outsourcer. Agreeing to the sources of the information and how they will be calculated is first and foremost in operational success. This must be a priority.
- Not adequately explaining metrics. This can be frustrating for the client when the metrics are not explained in detail or they keep changing due to inconsistently applied entries.

As soon as either of the parties realizes that any of the above behaviors are occurring or may occur, get together as a team and address them. None of these problems are insurmountable obstacles. Return to first principles and ask tough questions. Disregard what was done in the past and address the present and future. You may even want to hold more frequent roundtable discussions to work things out.

You can also prevent these behaviors and create a steady state in your relationship. The next section discusses how this can be done.

MARRIAGE TO FAMILY: A STEADY STATE FOR THE OUTSOURCING RELATIONSHIP

A marriage is more than a ceremony and a honeymoon. A marriage creates a family. The same can be said of an outsourcing relationship. There may be a formal agreement between two parties, but an outsourcing initiative and the relationship that you and your provider create can be bigger than its parts. Just as a family can get more done than a couple alone, so can you and your provider. It may not be as exciting as the ceremony or honeymoon, but the magnitude is still amazing.

What makes a happy family? The main thing is the ability to disagree while still trusting each other and getting along (putting aside personal differences). This means you and your provider must be flexible and be willing to compromise when a problem or unforeseen situation arises. Another characteristic of a happy family is the ability to keep the relationship fresh and not get into a rut. In an outsourcing relationship, this may mean reviewing the contract and making adjustments. Also, you and your provider should make note of things that worked in one facet of the project and see if they can be applied to other parts in the spirit of continuous improvement. You must also learn to deal with changes — in the project and in the relationship. Most outsourcing initiatives are long-term, and if you and your provider communicate well and challenge each other, you will be able to take changes and surprises in stride. The result will be a steady partnership that will take you from the honeymoon to a happy family preparing for a silver anniversary celebration.

---

1 Leslie Hansen Harps. "Logistics Outsourcing: Making a Long-Term Commitment," *Inbound Logistics,* July 2002. http://www.inboundlogistics.com/articles/features/0702_feature01.shtml.

2 http://www.saic.com/cover-archive/saicachieve/entergyOutsourcing.html.

ON THE ELEVATOR

Outsourcing relationships are between both organizations and people. Therefore, several types of relationships can form during and after implementation. The two most common are vendor/client and partnership. Ideally, you want your post-implementation relationship to move beyond vendor/client and toward partnership.

In many respects, the relationship between a company and an outsourcing provider is like the process of getting married. There is a courtship period that starts out with dating (the requirements and RFP process), followed by the wedding and honeymoon (selection, start-up, and the first months after start-up), and then, finally, a happy marriage (maintaining and managing the outsourcing relationship). The key is to maintain the atmosphere of teamwork and open communications that was established in the beginning.

As you begin building a lasting relationship with your provider, an important thing to remember is that there is no "off-the-shelf" approach. Establishing a relationship that is geared toward long-term success is as much an art as it is a science. The trick is communicating properly so that any disagreements become an impetus for moving the relationship and initiative forward. Therefore, you must adopt an acceptance mindset and agree to communicate openly and honestly with your outsourcing provider, so that your companies can build the lasting relationship necessary for outsourcing success. This includes:

- Establishing a regular, ongoing process for business planning, evolution and communications;
- Implementing a rewards structure of gain sharing or goal sharing;
- Making sure that there are regular, ongoing executive interactions;
- Reviewing the RFP and the contract after implementation and identifying surprises, changes, and problem areas;
- Measuring performance against the initial goals established for outsourcing;

- Conducting formal "lessons learned" roundtable meetings;
- Encouraging creativity and innovation on both sides of the relationship; and
- Building a lasting outsourcing relationship by emphasizing continuous improvement.

To create the right kind of outsourcing partnership, all organizational units within each company should be 100% directed towards the success of the outsourcing initiative. There can be no adversity between the outsourcer and provider. Instead, both you and your provider must function as a cohesive, collective whole. The goal is to eliminate the "we vs. they" problem that can undermine an outsourcing relationship. Once you have put a continuous improvement process in place, your relationship with your provider has a greater chance of growing, improving, and remaining strong. However, you can improve these chances even more by learning to recognize the signs that your relationship may be in trouble.

For the outsourcer, the behaviors that can lead to a failed initiative are:

- Poor executive communication;
- The elimination of daily relationships between managers of both parties;
- Failing to maintain metrics and monitor the relationship;
- Not accepting responsibility; and
- Using metrics as a whip and not a tool;

For the outsourcing provider, the following behaviors lead to trouble:

- Poor executive communication;
- Failure to be proactive;
- Not measuring and reporting performance;
- Not developing metrics with the outsourcer; and
- Not adequately explaining metrics.

As soon as either party realizes that any of the above behaviors are occurring or may occur, get together as a team and address them. None of these problems are insurmountable obstacles. Return to first principles and ask tough questions. Disregard what was done in the past and address the present and future. You may even want to hold more frequent roundtable discussions to work things out.

Most outsourcing initiatives are long-term, and if you and your provider communicate well and challenge each other, you will be able to take changes and surprises in stride. The result will be a steady partnership that will take you from the "honeymoon" to a happy family preparing for a silver anniversary celebration.

Managing the Relationship

INTRODUCTION

As we've already learned, establishing a successful outsourcing relationship is much like creating a happy marriage. By the same token, managing the ongoing relationship can be compared to taking care of a marriage so that you can get to your silver anniversary celebration. And this is not always so easy.

Some of the possible challenges an outsourcing relationship must overcome in the years that follow implementation include:

- The outsourcer's leadership or management changes, and the new people are not familiar with the outsourcing initiative or the operation;
- The outsourcing provider's on-site leadership changes (without notice or a clear plan);
- Mergers and acquisitions introduce new outsourcing alternatives;
- The outsourcing provider fails to evolve with the business;
- Operations do not focus on continuous improvement, and the relationship grows stale;
- Costs keep growing without any plan to contain or reduce the trend; or
- One side of the partnership does not invest the necessary time, effort, and resources into the success of the operation.

The keys to overcoming any or all of these challenges are leadership, continual communication, implementing change, and preparing for the future. This chapter demonstrates how to use these keys to ensure that the initiative thrives as time goes by and how to recognize the signs that your initiative is a success.

LEADERSHIP

Outsourcing relationship managers must be collaborative problem solvers who can address performance issues and results and discuss corrective action and the need for improvement, rather than telling those involved how to run the business. This is true not only of those who hold the title of relationship manager, but also of the leaders for both the outsourcer and the outsourcing provider. The leadership for all companies involved must show their ongoing commitment to the outsourcing relationship by staying actively involved and investing their time to keep it going. They must also:

- Champion change;
- Be good negotiators;
- Have excellent communication skills;
- Be the best at maintaining relationships; and
- Celebrate small successes.

The leadership responsibilities for the months and years after implementation are twofold: maintaining focus on the relationship and understanding that business changes. The sections that follow discuss these responsibilities in more detail.

Maintaining Focus on the Relationship

It is easy to get caught up in other activities, especially if the outsourcing initiative has been in place for some time; however, leaders must keep their eyes on the ball, or in this case, on the contract and the relationship. The best way to accomplish this is to:

- Review the contract often to verify that it is being followed or to see why it can no longer be followed;
- Not allow changes to go without notice or discussion;
- Make sure that the people involved do not forget about the relationship. Staff from your company and the provider's tend to get busy with their day-to-day routines and may need to be reminded that they are in this together. With leadership continuing to make this a focus, the relationship will continue to prosper;
- Maintain original meeting schedules. Also, you and your provider should hold ongoing relationship development meetings to advance the initiative to the next level and to make sure that you follow through on dates and timelines;

- Maintain a constant desire to make the agreement better for both parties;
- Develop and nurture a two-sided mindset for all issues; do not let an "us vs. them" mentality creep in and derail the relationship; and
- Maintain the open communications developed before, during and after implementation, as well as a spirit of compromise. Both parties must have ongoing strategic discussions to ensure that the relationship stays current and focused on the correct priorities. The point is to prevent surprises that can adversely affect the initiative, or even derail it.

Maintaining focus on the relationship should not be limited to the current dynamics. Leaders would be wise to consistently review how the relationship is functioning and suggest ways to improve its performance. How should service levels, budgets, and incentive plans be upgraded to make sure your relationship stays fresh? It is important that goals for the future of the relationship be established and that both the company and the provider accept these goals. A brighter future will not develop unless the leadership from all parties sets the pace.

Understanding that Business Changes

The function you outsourced goes through business cycles, just as all businesses do today. People in both companies change positions or move on; companies merge and acquire or are bought and sold. Two important questions for leaders to ask as these changes occur are: How is the relationship and performance holding up under the changing business climate? What changes need to be made to align the outsourcing relationship with the evolving requirements?

To proactively respond to change, leaders must:

- Be willing to change direction if the situation warrants it;
- Gracefully incorporate changes when needed;
- Recognize that customer demands change over time and work to ensure that the agreement and initiative are adjusted accordingly; and
- Support the implementation of process changes.

Then, to keep the outsourcing relationship on track, leaders should continually document changes and their effect on performance. For example, in a distribution outsourcing scenario, the profile of customer orders and inventory must be documented along with seasonal volume variations. Ideally, these profiles will be stated in the contract to serve as your starting point. Deviations from these profiles caused by business changes must be tracked and analyzed. For example, if a retailer elected to shift sales volume from their stores to direct-to-consumer Internet sales, then the volume and profile of customer orders will likely shift. Without a change in order processing — and possibly equipment and systems — the retailer's overall cost per order will go up even without any major increase in volume. Good outsourcing logistics providers can isolate those costs to help you do four things:

1. Understand distribution labor impacts;
2. Refine pricing for this new service;
3. Develop a joint plan to reduce costs and maintain service; and
4. Develop your operating budget for the next year;

Also, it is critical that both parties update all new people — whether they are executives or new members of the outsourcing team — with the correct history, data, and status of the relationship. The outsourcing team conducts these meetings, which should focus on the facts and not personal feelings. If necessary, you may want to share the contract with the appropriate new parties at the executive level.

Although it is important to review the contract to stay focused on the relationship and goals, if the contract continually becomes the point of reference in most discussions and meetings, it can signal several things about the contract:

• There are perception differences between the parties;
• There may be pricing problems on either side when behavior is justified by the contract (i.e., when either side is using the contract to justify or change pricing, this is a signal that someone is not happy with the agreement); or
• The contract may have become inadequate for the relationship and needs to be changed.

If one or all of these situations is present in your relationship, then it is time to address the possibility of upgrading service levels, budgets, and incentive plans (as mentioned in the previous section), along with confirming the perceptions of all parties. You and your provider may want to bring in your legal team to re-work the contract or establish new goals, services, and metrics.

Outsourcing Relationship Management: One Perspective

In a May 2004 interview, Michael Mah, a Senior Consultant with Cutter Consortium, addressed outsourcing relationship management. Here are some of his thoughts:

- There's no silver bullet in the relationship management arena. It's more of a continuous process, especially since you'll have to deal with turnover;
- What you're dealing with in this type of partnering is a fundamental shift in power that requires specific attention. If you do it well, both sides win; if you do it poorly, both sides can be damaged unnecessarily. And the financial cost of two damaged parties in a large-scale outsourcing relationship can be staggering. Not only in dollars, but in lost opportunity and bad publicity;
- You should have an ongoing program designed to maintain the principles of negotiation — negotiation on the merits. Here you're learning what's known as interest-based bargaining to create a win-win versus win-lose situation;
- A periodic training program is one method for making sure that negotiation principles are maintained. For example, you might consider a series of on-site workshops for both the sourcing teams and the executives on both sides to aim for good outcomes;
- A critical component in an outsourcing relationship is the joint creation of value. This will help you on two levels:

  1. On the project level, where negotiations happen weekly or even several times a week, and those people are often in conflict;
  2. At the executive level, where they are making contractual commitments between the large entities;

- Two partners who excel at outsourcing relationship management are going to be at a tremendous market advantage over two partners whose energy is being sapped by internal conflict. In the former scenario, both companies are focused on common problems in the marketplace, working as a team to focus on respective core competencies, bringing their gifts to the table, and aligning their skills and talents in ways that are mutually reinforcing. In the second scenario, you have people losing sight of solving problems and directing their energies at each other with tension and outright hostility, while the marketplace blows by them. The combination of relationship management, metrics, and good dispute resolution is really a competitive weapon.[1]

Continual Communication

The key to guaranteeing that changes do not upset the outsource relationship is open and continual communication between you and your outsourcing provider. Regular meetings foster open communications. This applies to all levels of the relationship, from company executives to those working in the outsourced function. Company executives from all parties, for example, should be involved in semi-annual relationship meetings. And leaders need to invest their time in strategic relationships.

On the outsourcing initiative and functions level, the relationship managers and outsourcing team should conduct regular meetings to:

- Update and review service levels;
- Update and review budgets and communicate positive and negative trends; and
- Update and review incentive plans based on the above and agree on improvement areas.

Continual communication should not stop at the doors of your company. Instead, the customers or users of the provider's services should be brought into the process of improving the outsourcing relationship. Hold customer focus meetings annually to gain an understanding of where your customers' business is going and to identify changes that need to be made to fulfill their needs. It would also be beneficial to invite your outsourcing provider to these meetings for a better understanding of customer expectations. After the customer focus meeting, you and your outsourcing provider must hold a planning meeting to determine how best to react to customer requests and to discuss process changes and implementation plans.

Throughout the life of your outsourcing relationship, constantly look for ways to work together and take advantage of opportunities inside and outside the operation. Both you and your outsourcing provider should be challenged to define opportunities to improve communications. This will build trust in the relationship and promote open problem solving.

Continual Communications: Questions to Ask

Below are some of the questions that Tompkins Associates encourages outsourcers to ask as part of a policy of open and regular communications:

- Are we following the contract? If not, is this good or bad?
- Are we following the timelines and responsibilities included in the contract? Is there room for improvement?
- How is the relationship and performance holding up under the changing business climate?
- What changes need to be made to align the outsourcing relationship with evolving requirements?
- What should we do to keep the relationship fresh and relevant?
- What are our goals for the future of our relationship? How can we make these our provider's goals?
- What can we do to improve communications?
- How can we achieve improvements in performance levels?
- How is the outsourcing relationship affecting customer perception of our company?
- What can we do to stay focused on the correct priorities?

IMPLEMENTING CHANGE

In a long-term relationship, change is inevitable. As mentioned earlier, the business you are outsourcing and the people involved will shift as time passes. You and your provider must be prepared to make adjustments to the process. If you have fostered continual communications as described in the last section, it will not be difficult to develop a process to implement changes.

The first step is to have a documented plan to provide a point of reference and help prevent surprises. While developing this plan, you should be certain that your company will be able to implement any changes on its end, as they can be the driving force for success.

The second step is to take your plan and put it in action. During this phase, it's important to monitor performance, cost and attitude. For example, be sensitive to cost increases due to change of operations. Again, your provider should identify these types of changes and bring them forward. Work with the provider on any solutions so that you will understand the magnitude of the increase and possibly assist with finding a way to decrease costs. Working together allows you to continue to understand each other's side of the business and the impacts of solutions on both organizations.

The third step is for both you and your provider to document what went right during the process change and what went wrong. Discuss both aspects, positive and negative, and look for ways to improve. This will also help you in future implementations because you may have to implement process changes several times over the life of your contract.

What if you encounter resistance to change from your outsourcing provider while you are either documenting or implementing your plan? This may signal an unwillingness to transform for the benefit of both parties. If this situation occurs, use the spirit of compromise to bring the reasons for this unwillingness to change to the surface. The reasons could be based on process or personality. If there is an issue about the process, you should review it and see if a few adjustments can end the provider's push back. If the reasons are based on personality or the other party is unwilling to compromise after the process review, involve a mediator with experience in overcoming these challenges.

PREPARING FOR THE FUTURE

All contracts have life spans. You should openly discuss the end of the contract term to let your provider know exactly what you expect. Developing the habit of continually documenting the relationship will prepare you for the end of the contract life and re-negotiation. It will also help you and your provider understand that although you may not be able to implement major changes and improvements under the current contract, they can be part of a renewed contract. As noted previously, distinguishing the changes that can take place under the current agreement and those that are best held off until the contract re-negotiation period is a process that requires the coordination of both parties. This period also presents a great opportunity to see how much of a partnership you have built. During the preparation for the end of the contract, both sides will be looking for improvements from their current position. The provider may desire more access to your business, and that means more business for them. On the other hand, you may want more flexibility and the ability to expand your network to other regions or countries. Both of these positions must be evaluated to answer the questions:

- Is this partner physically capable of undertaking this journey?
- Has this partner been flexible in responding to new requirements that will allow our business to grow?
- Do we as a business want to continue to work with this partner?

Part of preparing for the future involves considering the possibility that the contract will not be renewed once it has expired. As unpleasant as this option may be, it is one your company must be equipped to face. Make sure that you have a solid, documented plan for managing the exit and transfer costs.

SIGNS OF A SUCCESSFUL INITIATIVE

Earlier in this chapter, we covered the challenges that those involved in an outsourcing relationship must overcome to ensure success. However, it is just as important that we share the signs of a successful initiative — the rewards for excellent outsourcing relationship management. Basically, the signs are:

- All expectations are exceeded;
- All performance measures are made and the bar is raised;

- The outsourcing provider is invisible; in other words, the provider "looks like the client;"
- The end of the term is simply a renewal process; and
- Every success is celebrated in a fun environment.

These signs of victory are not easily achieved, but then, success is rarely easy. If your company and provider follow the steps and recommendations set forth here, it is likely that you will both be able to celebrate successes.

---

1 Michael Mah, Senior Consultant, "Ask the Experts," 2005, Cutter Consortium, Arlington, MA 02474, USA. http://www.cutter.com/consultants/mmbio.html.

ON THE ELEVATOR

Managing an outsourcing relationship for the long-term may be compared to taking care of a marriage so that you can get to your silver anniversary celebration. This is not easy. There are numerous challenges to overcome.

The keys to meeting these challenges and ensuring success in your outsourcing relationship are leadership, continual communication, implementing change, and preparing for the future. Leadership for all companies involved must demonstrate its ongoing commitment to the outsourcing relationship by staying actively involved and investing time to keep it going. Leaders should maintain focus on the relationship and understand that business will change over the life of the outsourcing agreement.

Successful management of an outsourcing relationship is the result of continual communications between all parties. The relationship managers and outsourcing team should conduct regular meetings to review and update service levels, budgets, and incentive plans. Company executives from both organizations need to hold semi-annual relationship meetings. You should also hold annual customer focus meetings to get an understanding of where your customers' business is going and to identify changes that need to be made to meet their needs. After the customer focus

meeting, you and your provider must hold a planning meeting to determine how best to react to customer requests and to discuss process changes and implementation plans.

In a long-term relationship, change is inevitable. You and your provider must be prepared to make adjustments to the process. If you have fostered continual communications, it will not be difficult to develop a process with your provider to implement changes. The first step is to have a documented plan. The second step is to take your plan and put it in action, all the while monitoring performance, cost and attitude. The third step is for both parties to document what went right during the process change and what went wrong so that you can better plan for the future.

All contracts have life spans, so openly discuss the end of the contract term to let your provider know what you expect. Part of preparing for the future includes considering the possibility that the contract will not be renewed once it has expired. Make sure that you have a solid, documented plan for managing the exit and transfer costs. And don't forget to share the signs of a successful initiative — the rewards for excellent outsourcing relationship management — and celebrate in a fun environment.

13 Mitigating Risk

The potential benefits of outsourcing are huge, but so are the potential hazards. To help you mitigate risk, here are the Top 40 Risks in outsourcing by the process steps: Strategy, Selection, Implementation and Management.

Outsourcing strategy is the process of determining whether or not to outsource and, if so, what to outsource. Outsourcing selection is the process of finding and evaluating potential outsourcing partners. Outsourcing implementation is where the relationship between outsourcing partners is defined and established. Outsourcing management is the monitoring and evolution of the ongoing relationship.

The process of Outsourcing Strategy (Chapters 4 and 5), Selection (Chapters 6 and 7), Implementation (Chapters 8–10), and Management (Chapters 11 and 12) is critical to achieving success. Each step comes with its own set of risks. Avoiding these risks via the robust outsourcing process presented in this book will significantly contribute to your ability to reap the rewards of outsourcing.

OUTSOURCING STRATEGY RISKS (CHAPTERS 4 AND 5)

1. Outsourcing undesirable functions versus the ones that provide the greatest competitive advantage;
2. Not clearly defining goals and objectives before starting the outsourcing process;
3. Not establishing an effective internal baseline against which providers are measured — including costs, service, and value adds;

4. Outsourcing in the international market without international operations experience;
5. Inadequate business-case development for the outsourcing decision;
6. Making the decision to outsource without complete information on internal costs and processes;
7. Not considering the impact of outsourcing on other functions and ignoring areas of risk such as environmental and regulatory factors;
8. Failure to understand human relations and employment law requirements for an outsourcing initiative;
9. Announcing outsourcing before sufficient details have been finalized, creating morale issues; and
10. Lack of risk analysis and risk assessment planning.

OUTSOURCING SELECTION RISKS (CHAPTERS 6 AND 7)

1. Not including enough resources to effectively manage the vendor selection process;
2. Lack of a proper internal skill set to effectively manage the selection process;
3. Not understanding or leveraging the benefits that a Request for Information (RFI) can have in narrowing the potential provider field before entering the Request for Proposal (RFP) process;
4. Not casting one's net widely enough for potential providers of the service, and thus missing good candidates;
5. Not involving a variety of perspectives in the selection process;
6. Using poorly developed and documented service or product specifications;
7. Inaccurate costing of assets that will be transferred to the service provider;
8. Not doing business and financial due diligence on potential providers;
9. Insufficient knowledge of service provider capacity limitations; and
10. Making the selection process a personal, rather than a commercial, decision.

OUTSOURCING IMPLEMENTATION RISKS (CHAPTERS 8–10)

1. Not establishing an outsourcing relationship that has sufficient flexibility to deal with business fluctuations;
2. Initiating an agreement with a service provider that limits flexibility in the future;
3. Having an unrealistic timeline for any of the steps of the outsource process, including start-up;
4. Poor implementation planning with respect to timing of transition to service provider and demands on the organization;
5. Underestimating the time required to negotiate a service agreement;
6. Not fully defining an employee transition plan;
7. Not getting the operational issues resolved in the service agreement before moving into the legal aspects of the agreement;
8. Inadequate planning concerning information systems and interfacing with the service provider;
9. Insufficient technology development before implementation; and
10. Not training the provider on critical elements of the company product line or on service expectations.

OUTSOURCING MANAGEMENT RISKS (CHAPTERS 11 AND 12)

1. Not considering the full impact of an outsourcing agreement on a company's financial condition;
2. Lack of internal communication;
3. Lack of incentives for provider continuous improvement;
4. Not establishing multiple touch points between the company and the provider;
5. Lack of a contingency plan for major disruptions at the service provider;
6. Not putting a full communication plan into effect, including escalation processes, regularly scheduled meetings, review periods, and employee communication;
7. Doing a poor job of managing expectations around the go-live;
8. Expecting too much from a provider in the early months after go-live;

9. Neglecting to "flex" the relationship as outsourcing requirements evolve; and

10. Lack of a formal "lessons learned" roundtable on outsourcing in general, and specifically, in established relationships.

Investing time and resources in the design and deployment of a proven outsourcing process will help you avoid the risks of outsourcing and move your organization forward to the next level of performance excellence.

Outsourcing Is Here To Stay

INTRODUCTION

In their ongoing search for increased competitiveness and success in today's global marketplace, companies are either considering outsourcing or they have already decided to pursue it. About 25% of the typical executive's budget currently goes to outsourcing supplies or services, and that is expected to increase to 34% by the end of 2006. There is no doubt that outsourcing can be a critical business solution; however, it is not something that happens magically. Outsourcing must be a core competency, just like any other important business process.

There is no evidence that the factors that made outsourcing a viable option are about to fade anytime soon. A strong, vibrant industry has developed to help manufacturing and logistics operations reduce costs by focusing on core functions. All the business challenges that have pushed companies toward outsourcing relationships still exist, as do all the benefits to be gained from a successful initiative. Moreover, the outsourcing partners available to help you pursue your own initiative are thriving.

But if an organization does not view outsourcing as a core competency, it becomes vulnerable to setbacks. In fact, outsourcing performed poorly can bring a business to its knees. On the other hand, outsourcing performed well can have tremendous payback. Use this solutions book as a guide in your pursuit for a successful outsourcing initiative, and you can avoid many of the pitfalls. This chapter is your call to action — we encourage you to make outsourcing a core competency using the proven methodology described here.

CALL TO ACTION

We have outlined the path to successfully define your core functions and processes, identify business targets, select outsourcing opportunities, determine with whom to partner, and build effective relationships. All that's left to do now is get started. You can move forward by:

- Sharing this book with your company's leadership and gaining their buy-in to the possibilities for improvement through outsourcing;
- Establishing a team to develop the outsourcing strategic plan;
- Defining the core functions and processes that present the best outsourcing opportunities. Primary core functions differentiate your company in the marketplace. Secondary core functions bring value to your customers, but at the same time, are not visible to them. Primary non-core functions affect your relationship with the customer but are not what your business is really all about. Secondary non-core functions are necessary for running your company but do not affect its success;
- Defining the appropriate business targets for the outsourcing function or process. It is prudent to conduct an internal baseline analysis and market research for each specific function. This will also help you identify internal process needs and service requirements, the cost structure of the candidates for outsourcing, and qualified providers that can meet your company's service and cost needs;
- Defining the path forward plan, including objectives, internal and external resources, and milestones to help guide the implementation team; and
- Following the procedures and processes outlined here to ensure a successful outsourcing implementation.

Those who have made the commitment to read this book and learn from our years of experience with outsourcing wins and losses must be willing to take the next step and put their plan into action. If you apply the wealth of knowledge within these pages, you will be triumphant in opening the door for future operational improvements. We wish you well as you work to make outsourcing a part of your long-term improvement strategy. We would also like to remind you that if you are still in doubt about how to pursue an outsourcing initiative, you could also leverage the expertise of proven outsourcing process consultants. With the proper planning, great benefits will follow.

GO! GO! GO!

Appendix: On the Elevator

Have you ever been on an elevator with an important business colleague and wished you could quickly and eloquently communicate your thoughts? This "On the Elevator" summary from the end of each chapter will help you make the best use of the three-minute elevator ride. Photo copy this section to hand out to your outsourcing team for a complete checklist of all the bases to cover when you begin your outsourcing initiative.

CHAPTER 1 — LOGISTICS AND MANUFACTURING OUTSOURCING

Outsourcing is a management tool that shifts the organizational structure of companies. It is a business transformation process that can create great opportunity for improved performance, but it can also create great opportunity for problems, issues, and, ultimately, failure. While outsourcing is a relatively new term, the idea has been around for a long time. It was a part of doing business in Renaissance Italy and 19th century England.

After World War II, it fell out of favor as companies transformed themselves into vertical enterprises, trying to be all things to all people. But in the last few decades and particularly in the last 10 years, trends such as downsizing, right-sizing, consolidating, and reengineering combined with the explosion of the Internet have shifted the focus of company leaders back to outsourcing. Software and technology offerings have expanded, new products and innovations have grown, and management's thinking has shifted to an understanding that some assets are costly and can hurt earnings.

As a result, more and more companies are eyeing outsourcing as a viable method for improving speed to market and increasing market share. The percentage of budgets spent on outsourcing is rising, providers are becoming more capable, contractors are experiencing heightened competition, and the percentage of companies outsourcing manufacturing and logistics services is on a sharp increase. This is a new development, except in the small electronics manufacturing sector. Until now, the focus of outsourcing has been HR, IT, and marketing. This is obvious if you do any kind of search on the Web for outsourcing. It is also the reason we have decided to write this book. Look at it this way: many of the most profitable, well-known, and highly touted companies have gotten where they are by outsourcing logistics and manufacturing.

So, with all the stories of outsourcing success and the excitement they generate, it's no wonder that so many companies are either already outsourcing or plan to outsource in the next year. However, in the search for core competencies and non-core competencies to outsource, it's easy to overlook the fact that outsourcing itself is a competency. As such, it must be approached with business process knowledge and effective outsourcing process experience to reap its full benefits. It also requires a thorough understanding of today's business challenges and how outsourcing can be used effectively to manage them.

CHAPTER 2 — TODAY'S BUSINESS CHALLENGES

Business is not as much fun as it used to be. There's too much to do and not enough time to do it. Competition, globalization, technology, pace, and the capital markets have all had a major impact on business today, creating the following challenges:

- Shifting channel structures and business relationships — Today's company has morphed into a diversified entity that competes, collaborates, and co-creates in a network of other companies. These entities strive to become virtual organizations. They are forging new relationships, enhancing their supply chains, increasing organizational responsiveness and focusing on bottom line results. Ultimately, those who truly understand how to nurture partnerships, such as relationships with their external suppliers and service providers, will triumph. This is the challenge of business relationships and shifting channel structures;
- Customer satisfaction — Customization, customer value, customer control, customer relationship management, and customer-centric thinking are increasingly being used to describe business focus. This requires companies to divest themselves of self-interest and

concentrate on the needs, expectations, and perceptions of those
who buy and use their products. What happens when customers'
thoughts, wants, and needs drive innovation and flow of goods
and services from raw materials suppliers to retailers and ultimately
back to those customers? You have customer satisfaction. These
requirements are not to be taken lightly; they require a great deal
of effort and intense cooperation;

- Speeding time to market — Today's business environment demands
  speed and more speed. The key to increasing speed to market is the
  creation of multilevel networks with a view to reducing customer
  lead-time, production lead-time, and manufacturing lead-time.
  These networks are complex, created through partnerships with
  suppliers, outsourcing providers, and third parties. They must be
  flexible, meeting all customer satisfaction requirements through
  robust design methods enabled by real-time decision tools and manufacturing and distribution synthesis. The networks must be built
  carefully, with the correct balance of insourcing and outsourcing;

- Information technology — With information technology, companies can extend their market reach and accomplish things beyond
  the scope of imagination. However, they can also make costly
  mistakes if they do not use it wisely or properly. It's important to
  remember that IT will not solve a company's ills by itself, but instead is a critical tool to be applied judiciously so that it facilitates
  communication between different groups and companies;

- Globalization — New trade agreements, individual countries partnering with each other to produce and export goods, international
  e-commerce, and Web applications have created a 24/7, on-
  demand, global marketplace. Politics and technology took us down
  this path, but the current focus on reducing costs and increasing
  profits has cemented it into a requirement for doing business today.
  To answer the challenge of globalization, companies must be aware
  of when to take advantage of what it has to offer and to think carefully about its impacts on customer satisfaction;

- Virtual factories — Virtual factories are the product of focused
  factories, deverticalization, the ease of sharing information all over
  the world, the Web, outsourcing, globalization, and the demand
  for increasing speed to market. The transformation of huge, outdated manufacturing monoliths into these sleek, lean, flexible,
  and agile operations presents a major challenge.

- Outsourcing — Today's most unique business challenge is outsourcing because it is both a solution to other business challenges and a challenge in its own right. Numerous companies have had considerable success with outsourcing secondary non-core functions (audit, landscaping, payroll, food services, janitorial, etc.), and so a logical extension is to pursue primary non-core functions (logistics, information technology, marketing, manufacturing, etc.). For outsourcing to work, a solid, up-front effort is required to identify the functions to be outsourced, so that the right processes that have the best returns are considered. Once the identification has been completed, then an organization's outsourcing process must be rigorously applied to assure that the potential benefits of outsourcing are achieved. This is the real challenge of outsourcing — making it a core competency so that it truly is a solution for other business challenges. When you do this, outsourcing is no longer a challenge, but an opportunity.

Chapter 3 — The Outsourcing Opportunity

In the days when vertical enterprises were the norm, operations functions were handled in-house. In the past two decades, however, keeping all operations in-house has become a burden. Outsourcing operations is a method that lets someone else carry that burden. By using contract manufacturers, third-party logistics providers, or a combination of both, companies can streamline production and distribution.

There are risks to outsourcing. Stories of failed outsourcing initiatives abound. But, if you know how to approach outsourcing or work with someone who fully understands the outsourcing process and has made it a core competency, the benefits far outweigh the risks. When done properly, outsourcing primary non-core operations functions yields a wealth of benefits — those with direct impact on a company and those that are not as obvious but affect the services that remain in-house. Direct benefits include:

- Focus on core competency;
- Reduction in manufacturing and logistics costs through the consolidation of operations and reduction of inventory carrying and transportation costs;
- Reduction in management and hourly head count;

- Improved accuracy through better inventory visibility and production tracking;
- Flexibility and wider range of service;
- Access to global networks and superior technology (world-class WMS, TMS, MES, OMS) results in the collaboration that consolidates loads, and allows smaller organizations to share space, IT support, and operation;
- Improved service through shorter order cycle time, visibility of available inventory, and accountability;
- Improved quality resulting from less damage, less scrap, and improved response time to inquiries; and
- Reduction in capital investment and increased cash infusion because facilities are no longer on the balance sheet and assets can be sold.

The indirect benefits of operations outsourcing are:

- Creating a catalyst for change by highlighting how outsourced operations are managed;
- Initiating or fueling expansion by allowing a company to offer new services because outsourcing has improved performance;
- Stimulating analysis due to the requirement to document business processes and their costs;
- Converting sluggish functional areas into dynamic, successful ones; and
- Developing resources and contacts brought to the table by the service provider.

The key to taking advantage of all outsourcing has to offer lies in your outsourcing strategy — defining your core competencies, defining targets, and managing your outsourcing relationships.

CHAPTER 4 — DEFINING CORE

Before beginning the important task of defining core processes, you must understand your company's goals and have a strategic vision and plan in place. To grasp company goals, leaders should ask themselves these questions:

- Where is the company headed?
- How will we get there?
- What is the science of our business?

- What values will be practiced?
- How will we measure success?

By addressing the "Where" portion of the goals, leaders can create the company's strategic vision. When company leaders work to answer the "How" portion of their company's goals, they are also defining the company's strategic plan, or mission. Completing these tasks makes it easier for company leaders to step back, evaluate the results, and then set about defining the company's core competency.

The process of defining "Core" requires awareness of the four types of business functions within a company — primary core, secondary core, primary non-core, and secondary non-core. Primary core functions are the things that differentiate your company in the marketplace, and more importantly, they are the reasons your customers come to you. Secondary core functions are those things that bring value to your customer and must be done well, but at the same time, they are not visible to your customer. Primary non-core functions are those that can affect your relationship with your customer but are not what your business is about. Secondary non-core functions are those processes that are necessary for running the business but do not affect your company's success.

To properly define "core," develop a team made up of company leaders who understand the strategic nature of the vision. Breaking the company up into discrete processes is one of the first tasks this group must undertake. These discrete processes will become more defined further down the road and may be consolidated or divided even further, depending on the availability of external service providers. This task helps break down the decision into manageable chunks.

Once this process is complete, the discussion of defining "core" can begin. There are some definite questions that must be asked in order to understand and evaluate "core." These questions are:

- Who are our customers?
- How do the functions we have defined touch the customer? Or do they touch the customer?
- What is it that our customers know us for most?
- What is it that our company does that provides the most value to the customer?
- What is it that we do that may be difficult for our competitors to imitate?

Answering all of these questions for each of the business processes you have defined will help you understand if they are core functions. Once you have defined "core" and its supporting processes, there needs to be consensus around which functions to evaluate for outsourcing.

CHAPTER 5 — DEFINING OUTSOURCING TARGETS

Most outsourcing decisions are based on the economic returns or savings compared to the cost. However, the real reason companies should outsource is the need to focus management time and resources. A clear side benefit of outsourcing is cost savings and service improvements, but the real driver needs to be management focus.

Companies must focus management time and attention on their core competencies and maintain efforts to continuously improve those functions that are core. A look at organizations' histories shows the deterioration in performance that occurs when company leaders and managers begin to focus on non-core activities. Profit performance declines and competitiveness weakens. Therefore, functions that are outside of the core should be outsourced to free management time and organizational resources to work on the highest priority activities — core competencies.

To select specific functions for outsourcing, an internal baseline analysis and market research initiative is required. This process will also help the company identify:

- Internal needs and service requirements for the functions or processes;
- The cost structure of the functions or processes that are candidates for outsourcing;
- Qualified providers that can meet the service and cost needs of the company.

Rushing the baseline development step can cause serious consequences to the future of the company, resulting in poor outsourcing selection decisions, a decline in performance, and an increase in costs.

A baselining and market research initiative has five basic components. They are:

- Establishing a Baseline Analysis Team — This team is responsible for collecting the data, analyzing it, and preparing baseline summary documents for each function;

- Defining data requirements and analysis methodology — This definition process starts with the development of a list of the data required to fully document *each* current function or process. Then, the team must identify the appropriate method for collecting data, performing the analysis, and reporting the results. The goal of these steps is to understand the current functions, determine current requirements, develop high-level selection criteria, and get steering team agreement;
- Developing a baseline model — The baseline model is used to validate existing functional processes. It involves collecting data about the processes, mapping the business processes, developing issues lists, developing cost and service level baselines, comparing internal baselines against industry best practices for validation, and preparing a summary document for each process considered a candidate for outsourcing;
- Performing market evaluation of service providers — This is accomplished by identifying potential providers, preparing RFIs for high-level due diligence of available providers, and evaluating the RFI responses to identify potential service providers based on selection criteria; and
- Developing specific outsourcing recommendations — In this step, the team determines the feasibility of outsourcing specific functions or processes based on the work it has done, identifies those functions or processes that meet company financial return objectives, prioritizes the list of potential outsource providers, obtains consensus on the prioritized list, and prepares for the next steps in the outsourcing process.

CHAPTER 6 — THE SOLICITATION PROCESS

Once your outsourcing team has identified primary and secondary core processes and determined its outsourcing targets, it is time to solicit providers for the processes being outsourced. This is one of the most critical components of the outsourcing process, and it must be done properly. To prepare an RFP that will allow you to select the best provider, you must take the following actions:

- Clearly set forth the goals to be achieved by outsourcing, keeping in mind that your primary goal will be to return leadership and management focus to the levels necessary for peak performance. Do not assume that today's level of performance is what is required for the service provider. The goals must fit the organization's needs over the life of the relationship.

- Develop a detailed, realistic timeline for the outsource process. Identify key dates such as RFP release, RFP response, site visits, short list, due diligence, selection, term sheet signing, contract signing, beginning implementation, and completing implementation.

- Involve senior management early, often, and at key decision points. Be certain senior management understands the scope, goals and timeline. Set realistic expectations. Obtain leadership support.

- Be certain that a wide range of candidates are pre-qualified before sending the RFP. Consider outsource providers as well as industry players. Perform extensive research to be certain all viable candidates are asked to bid by creating an RFI that clearly defines your needs and evaluating the responses to those needs.

- Clearly define the scope of what is to be outsourced. Once the scope is defined be sure that the boundaries of what is to be outsourced are clearly established.

- Establish benchmarks for the cost of self-performing and expected service levels that will serve as a baseline for the outsourced activity.

- Be certain the RFP provides a clear set of requirements, a clear path forward, and a clear desire for innovation and creativity. Use the RFP to tell people what needs to be done. Do not use the RFP to tell potential providers how to do their jobs. Be certain the full range of volume requirements is set forth to include slow, typical, and high levels of activity.

- Share the outsourcing process and timeline with each qualified provider. Be sure all candidates are given the same information and opportunity to present their best bid.

CHAPTER 7 — REQUEST FOR PROPOSAL AND SERVICE PROVIDER SELECTION

Evaluating proposals and choosing your final candidate is a time-consuming process. A key thing to keep telling yourself is "Success is all in the details." You must stay focused and consider all angles when you evaluate proposals.

Here are some tips for a successful evaluation:

- Deciding who will do the evaluation is as important as how to do it. The team that will do the evaluation should come from a variety of different "touch points" with the outsourced function. This cross-functional team should have a good understanding of the function being outsourced and should ultimately be involved with the outsource provider in some capacity. A word of caution: having the wrong people involved in the selection can easily result in making the wrong decision. Be sure to exclude people with an up-front bias.

- It is important to control communications with all potential providers while the evaluation process is ongoing. A single point of contact should be communicating with the potential providers. All providers should be given the same information and all questions and answers to the providers should be handled through the contact.

- The evaluation process is a business decision, not a low-cost or a personal preference. The process must be methodical. Relationships and executive preferences should not be overly emphasized. The evaluation criteria must be rigorously applied in a fair and equitable manner.

- The evaluation process should not be rushed. Often, time pressures are present, but these pressures should not result in the team allowing the process to be anything other than fair, detailed, and robust.

- Have a clear understanding of how your team will be handling short list determination, second visits, and additional information requests. Be sure the short list process is followed and the evaluation team and process are maintained through the short list and ultimate selection process.

- Be sure to evaluate proposals and not sales presentations. The written bid is what should be evaluated. In a similar way, you must evaluate the potential provider's company as a whole and not its sales team.

- Bids are often complex. Be sure all bids address the full scope of the functions to be outsourced. Be sure the evaluation is "apples to apples" and "oranges to oranges." Examine the details of the pricing and do the arithmetic on the pricing proposal for benchmark levels. Do not make assumptions or take the bids at face value.

- Contact at least three customers of each potential provider and obtain insights into the provider's performance. Ask a standard set of questions and be certain to obtain provider feedback on everything that gives you concern. If appropriate, go visit customers and view their performance first-hand.
- Until a binding relationship is established, you should always retain more than one provider option. Therefore, do not tell any potential provider they are "the winner" until after a binding term sheet or contract is signed. For larger outsourced contracts, it is appropriate to hold detailed, binding term sheet discussions with more than one potential provider.

Chapter 8 — Creating the Outsourcing Relationship

Outsourcing is giving up internal control of a business function and trusting others to handle this function for you. Therefore, the relationship between you and your outsourcing provider cannot be taken lightly. Although you may have built a great relationship during the selection process, this is not the outsourcing relationship that will take you through your initiative. Creating the outsourcing relationship involves:

- Getting the relationship started — A failed relationship can lead to complicated and costly legal battles. Therefore, as soon as is practicable, you should create a new team — the implementation team — comprised of members of both companies to begin the process of creating your relationship. This includes setting initial expectations, identifying resources in advance, determining where you are now and your destination, defining the relationship desired, and planning for resistance.
- Determining the relationship structure — Structure is important. Without a strong relationship structure, your initiative will lack control. Customer satisfaction, communication, and understanding of the business scope will be poor or nonexistent. Technology will most likely be inadequate and the management of the initiative will become reactive rather than proactive. Therefore, once you have started your relationship, you must determine what structure will work best.
- Selecting a fee structure — Fee structures should be as flexible as the relationships that create them. At the highest level, the pricing

(fee) options are: fixed-cost, transactional fee, cost-plus, activity-based, management fee, and combined structures. Each option has advantages and disadvantages. It is important that both you and your provider explore each option before you decide which you will apply to your initiative.

- Validation (relationship due diligence) — During validation, a client and a provider work together as a team to understand what the other is selling and what it needs. Both must be prepared to change assumptions or make adjustments to their expectations.
- Setting realistic timeline expectations — Before you and your provider get involved in the legal issues necessary for cementing your relationship, you need to develop a realistic and detailed timeline. This creates common thinking about the process and the next steps.

This process is not always going to be perfect, but there are a few things you can keep in mind as you work together to help it along:

- Do not over-promise on either side;
- Share information;
- Analyze available data, understand that it is likely to be historical, and deal with data gaps and integrity;
- Tour sites to see them with your own eyes;
- Do not make unfounded assumptions; and
- Line up all levels and functional groups from both organizations.

Most importantly, make sure that you ask a lot of questions and en- courage the provider to do the same. Although this is not rocket science, it is complex. The more questions you ask and answer, the better off your relationship will be.

CHAPTER 9 — SUCCESSFUL OUTSOURCING RELATIONSHIPS: A LEGAL PERSPECTIVE

Involve experienced outsourcing counsel early. Your legal team needs time to understand the drivers behind your decision to outsource and what your goals are for the outsourcing initiative. It is best to involve the legal team before or during the RFI step to improve your selection process. Your counsel will then be familiar with all the players and can contribute to the selection process. This also better prepares the legal team when it is time to negotiate.

Your legal team's outsourcing negotiation strategies should include understanding your company's negotiating position and objectives in the outsourcing initiative. To accomplish this, make sure your counsel has the answers to the following questions:

- What is driving the decision to outsource — commercial, financial, technological?
- What departments are impacted and what are the consequences to each?
- How can the objectives be utilized in negotiations with the provider?

You and your legal team should also decide whether to wait until you have selected one final provider (sole source) before you start the negotiations or to begin the negotiation process with two finalists (negotiating in parallel).

It is best to lead the negotiations with a binding term sheet, which allows you to settle on the terms of the deal without bogging down the parties involved in "legalese." The negotiated term sheet embodies the deal and will be the basis of the agreement. Properly constructed, it makes preparation, negotiation, and execution of the definitive agreement a simple process and allows you to continue to evaluate and improve the service provider's proposed charges, technical solutions, and legal terms.

At minimum, the term sheet must:

- Integrate commercial, legal, technical, and financial issues;
- Balance risk and reward;
- Balance certainty and flexibility;
- Provide price predictability; and
- Plan for exit.

The contract terms that will be the subject of a great deal of discussion between your company, the legal team, and the provider are *service levels* and *performance measures*. The service level part of the agreement must identify each service level clearly and objectively. Performance measures are usually included with service levels. These are performance indicators that are aligned with your strategic direction, are appropriate to the project, and provide readily understood signals of when the provider is succeeding and when improvement is needed. A common practice is to include a provision for benchmarks against which you and your provider periodically compare services and prices with industry best practices. This requires looking outside your organization for best-in-class performance comparisons and comparing your business with companies within and outside your industry. Many consulting groups and research organizations have developed formal benchmarking data and offer it as a product for this purpose.

For each portion of the term sheet, it is important that you, your counsel, and the provider expend energy to make sure everything is clearly stated and that all issues are understood. Once you have done this, all parties will have a solid foundation for drafting the final contract and executing the service agreement.

CHAPTER 10 — GETTING STARTED: PUTTING THE OUTSOURCING RELATIONSHIP IN MOTION

The period of transition from selection through implementation is underestimated, taken for granted, and not given enough effort. Work hard to prevent this from happening. Both parties must be able to understand and accept the fact that you are dealing with new people and a new culture and be prepared to make adjustments.

During this time, you and your chosen outsourcing provider must also be aware of and avoid the following major outsourcing relationship pitfalls:

- Unrealistic goals;
- False perceptions; and
- Lowered expectations.

The negative results of these pitfalls are non-performance, cost increases, and failure to achieve continuous improvement. To prevent these difficulties, you should define and manage expectations, develop metrics, conduct roundtables with senior management, and review your transition plan often.

Another important consideration: who will manage the relationship?

The relationship manager should be chosen by both parties. Technical ability is not as important as the ability to lead, make difficult decisions, and manage others.

During the transition period from selection to start-up, teams should be built to foster communication and knowledge transition. These teams should consist of members from your company and the provider's. Both you and the provider should also make sure that any teams you create within your organizations mirror one another, and you should decide whether each of you should have a project manager or if one project manager from the provider's company will suffice.

Establishing rules of engagement will facilitate the relationship. Some of the questions to consider are: how often to meet, who will be involved in start-up and transition, how each party will treat the other, what is strictly forbidden, and what hierarchy will be used for problem escalation? Answering these questions will allow you and your provider to establish the rules of engagement, as well as the roles and responsibilities of your company and theirs.

Develop a solid communications plan that focuses on the quality of information shared. The first step is to set clear communication expectations up-front. Decide early on who is going to communicate what to whom and when. Then, as you would with any other part of the project roll-out, document those communications requirements in the form of a plan and publish it.

Other guidelines for a successful start up are:

- Gain senior management buy-in and commitment;
- Agree to be open;
- Create a joint sign-off process;
- Celebrate small successes along the way;
- Do not keep the initiative a secret;
- Solve problems as they arise; and
- Create a timeline and stick to it.

CHAPTER 11 — ESTABLISHING THE ONGOING RELATIONSHIP

Outsourcing relationships are between both organizations and people. Therefore, several types of relationships can form during and after implementation. The two most common are vendor/client and partnership. Ideally, you want your post-implementation relationship to move beyond vendor/client and toward partnership.

In many respects, the relationship between a company and an outsourcing provider is like the process of getting married. There is a courtship period that starts out with dating (the requirements and RFP process), followed by the wedding and honeymoon (selection, start-up, and the first months after start-up), and then, finally, a happy marriage (maintaining and managing the outsourcing relationship). The key is to maintain the atmosphere of teamwork and open communications that was established in the beginning.

As you begin building a lasting relationship with your provider, an important thing to remember is that there is no "off-the-shelf" approach. Establishing a relationship that is geared toward long-term success is as much an art as it is a science. The trick is communicating properly so that any disagreements become an impetus for moving the relationship and initiative forward. Therefore, you must adopt an acceptance mindset and agree to communicate openly and honestly with your outsourcing provider, so that your companies can build the lasting relationship necessary for outsourcing success. This includes:

- Establishing a regular, ongoing process for business planning, evolution and communications;
- Implementing a rewards structure of gain sharing or goal sharing;
- Making sure that there are regular, ongoing executive interactions;
- Reviewing the RFP and the contract after implementation and identifying surprises, changes, and problem areas;
- Measuring performance against the initial goals established for outsourcing;
- Conducting formal "lessons learned" roundtable meetings;
- Encouraging creativity and innovation on both sides of the relationship; and
- Building a lasting outsourcing relationship by emphasizing continuous improvement.

To create the right kind of outsourcing partnership, all organizational units within each company should be 100% directed towards the success of the outsourcing initiative. There can be no adversity between the outsourcer and provider. Instead, both you and your provider must function as a cohesive, collective whole. The goal is to eliminate the "we vs. they" problem that can undermine an outsourcing relationship. Once you have put a continuous improvement process in place, your relationship with your provider has a greater chance of growing, improving, and remaining strong. However, you can improve these chances even more by learning to recognize the signs that your relationship may be in trouble.

For the outsourcer, the behaviors that can lead to a failed initiative are:

- Poor executive communication;
- The elimination of daily relationships between managers of both parties;

- Failing to maintain metrics and monitor the relationship;
- Not accepting responsibility; and
- Using metrics as a whip and not a tool;

For the outsourcing provider, the following behaviors lead to trouble:

- Poor executive communication;
- Failure to be proactive;
- Not measuring and reporting performance;
- Not developing metrics with the outsourcer; and
- Not adequately explaining metrics.

As soon as either party realizes that any of the above behaviors are occurring or may occur, get together as a team and address them. None of these problems are insurmountable obstacles. Return to first principles and ask tough questions. Disregard what was done in the past and address the present and future. You may even want to hold more frequent roundtable discussions to work things out.

Most outsourcing initiatives are long-term, and if you and your provider communicate well and challenge each other, you will be able to take changes and surprises in stride. The result will be a steady partnership that will take you from the "honeymoon" to a happy family preparing for a silver anniversary celebration.

CHAPTER 12 — MANAGING THE RELATIONSHIP

Managing an outsourcing relationship for the long-term may be compared to taking care of a marriage so that you can get to your silver anniversary celebration. This is not easy. There are numerous challenges to overcome.

The keys to meeting these challenges and ensuring success in your outsourcing relationship are leadership, continual communication, implementing change, and preparing for the future. Leadership for all companies involved must demonstrate its ongoing commitment to the outsourcing relationship by staying actively involved and investing time to keep it going. Leaders should maintain focus on the relationship and understand that business will change over the life of the outsourcing agreement.

Successful management of an outsourcing relationship is the result of continual communications between all parties. The relationship managers and outsourcing team should conduct regular meetings to review and update service levels, budgets, and incentive plans. Company executives from both organizations need to hold semi-annual relationship meetings. You should also hold annual customer focus meetings to get an understanding of where your customers' business is going and to identify changes that need to be made to meet their needs. After the customer focus meeting, you and your provider must hold a planning meeting to determine how best to react to customer requests and to discuss process changes and implementation plans.

In a long-term relationship, change is inevitable. You and your provider must be prepared to make adjustments to the process. If you have fostered continual communications, it will not be difficult to develop a process with your provider to implement changes. The first step is to have a documented plan. The second step is to take your plan and put it in action, all the while monitoring performance, cost and attitude. The third step is for both parties to document what went right during the process change and what went wrong so that you can better plan for the future.

All contracts have life spans, so openly discuss the end of the contract term to let your provider know what you expect. Part of preparing for the future includes considering the possibility that the contract will not be renewed once it has expired. Make sure that you have a solid, documented plan for managing the exit and transfer costs. And don't forget to share the signs of a successful initiative — the rewards for excellent outsourcing relationship management — and celebrate in a fun environment.

Chapter 13 — Mitigating Risk

The process of Outsourcing Strategy (Chapters 4 and 5), Selection (Chapters 6 and 7), Implementation (Chapters 8–10), and Management (Chapters 11 and 12) is critical to achieving success. Each step comes with its own set of risks. Avoiding these risks via the robust outsourcing process presented in this book will significantly contribute to your ability to reap the rewards of outsourcing.

Outsourcing Strategy Risks (Chapters 4 and 5)

1. Outsourcing undesirable functions versus the ones that provide the greatest competitive advantage;
2. Not clearly defining goals and objectives before starting the outsourcing process;
3. Not establishing an effective internal baseline against which providers are measured — including costs, service, and value adds;

4. Outsourcing in the international market without international operations experience;
5. Inadequate business-case development for the outsourcing decision;
6. Making the decision to outsource without complete information on internal costs and processes;
7. Not considering the impact of outsourcing on other functions and ignoring areas of risk such as environmental and regulatory factors;
8. Failure to understand human relations and employment law requirements for an outsourcing initiative;
9. Announcing outsourcing before sufficient details have been finalized, creating morale issues; and
10. Lack of risk analysis and risk assessment planning.

Outsourcing Selection Risks (Chapters 6 and 7)

1. Not including enough resources to effectively manage the vendor selection process;
2. Lack of a proper internal skill set to effectively manage the selection process;
3. Not understanding or leveraging the benefits that a Request for Information (RFI) can have in narrowing the potential provider field before entering the Request for Proposal (RFP) process;
4. Not casting one's net widely enough for potential providers of the service, and thus missing good candidates;
5. Not involving a variety of perspectives in the selection process;
6. Using poorly developed and documented service or product specifications;
7. Inaccurate costing of assets that will be transferred to the service provider;
8. Not doing business and financial due diligence on potential providers;
9. Insufficient knowledge of service provider capacity limitations; and
10. Making the selection process a personal, rather than a commercial, decision.

Outsourcing Implementation Risks (Chapters 8–10)

1. Not establishing an outsourcing relationship that has sufficient flexibility to deal with business fluctuations;

2. Initiating an agreement with a service provider that limits flexibility in the future;

3. Having an unrealistic timeline for any of the steps of the outsource process, including start-up;

4. Poor implementation planning with respect to timing of transition to service provider and demands on the organization;

5. Underestimating the time required to negotiate a service agreement;

6. Not fully defining an employee transition plan;

7. Not getting the operational issues resolved in the service agreement before moving into the legal aspects of the agreement;

8. Inadequate planning concerning information systems and interfacing with the service provider;

9. Insufficient technology development before implementation; and

10. Not training the provider on critical elements of the company product line or on service expectations.

Outsourcing Management Risks (Chapters 11 and 12)

1. Not considering the full impact of an outsourcing agreement on a company's financial condition;

2. Lack of internal communication;

3. Lack of incentives for provider continuous improvement;

4. Not establishing multiple touch points between the company and the provider;

5. Lack of a contingency plan for major disruptions at the service provider;

6. Not putting a full communication plan into effect, including escalation processes, regularly scheduled meetings, review periods, and employee communication;

7. Doing a poor job of managing expectations around the go-live;

8. Expecting too much from a provider in the early months after go-live;

9. Neglecting to "flex" the relationship as outsourcing requirements evolve; and

10. Lack of a formal "lessons learned" roundtable on outsourcing in general, and specifically, in established relationships.

CHAPTER 14 — OUTSOURCING IS HERE TO STAY

We have outlined the path to successfully define your core functions and processes, identify business targets, select outsourcing opportunities, determine with whom to partner, and build effective relationships. All that's left to do now is get started. You can move forward by:

- Sharing this book with your company's leadership and gaining their buy-in to the possibilities for improvement through outsourcing;
- Establishing a team to develop the outsourcing strategic plan;
- Defining the core functions and processes that present the best outsourcing opportunities. *Primary core functions* differentiate your company in the marketplace. *Secondary core functions* bring value to your customers, but at the same time, are not visible to them. *Primary non-core functions* affect your relationship with the customer but are not what your business is really all about. *Secondary non-core functions* are necessary for running your company but do not affect its success;
- Defining the appropriate business targets for the outsourcing function or process. It is prudent to conduct an internal baseline analysis and market research for each specific function. This will also help you identify internal process needs and service requirements, the cost structure of the candidates for outsourcing, and qualified providers that can meet your company's service and cost needs;
- Defining the path forward plan, including objectives, internal and external resources, and milestones to help guide the implementation team; and
- Following the procedures and processes outlined here to ensure a successful outsourcing implementation.

Those who have made the commitment to read this book and learn from our years of experience with outsourcing wins and losses must be willing to take the next step and put their plan into action. If you apply the wealth of knowledge within these pages, you will be triumphant in opening the door for future operational improvements. We wish you well as you work to make outsourcing a part of your long-term improvement strategy. We would also like to remind you that if you are still in doubt about how to pursue an outsourcing initiative, you could also leverage the expertise of proven outsourcing process consultants. With the proper planning, great benefits will follow.

GO! GO! GO!

Index

ABOUT TOMPKINS ASSOCIATES

From our beginning over 30 years ago, Tompkins has offered clients long-term solutions that accommodate companies' changing needs and provide the foundation for future growth. With an emphasis on integrated solutions, Tompkins' expertise provides the understanding that can guide companies to Supply Chain Excellence. Tompkins Associates develops and implements strategies for intelligent solutions in distribution center design, warehouse strategic planning, distribution network configuration, transportation system planning, system integration and implementation, logistics and manufacturing outsourcing, and supply chain optimization.

Tompkins offers a proven track record and deep industry expertise for solutions that reduce costs and improve overall supply chain performance.

With corporate headquarters located in Raleigh, North Carolina, Tompkins Associates has offices in Florida, Georgia, California, North Carolina, Canada, and the United Kingdom. For more information, visit our website at www.tompkinsinc.com.

TOMPKINS
ASSOCIATES
30 Years ✦ 1975-2005

May, 2005

ABOUT TOMPKINS PRESS

Established in 1997, Tompkins Press is dedicated to providing readers with the latest information on Supply Chain Excellence through leading-edge publications that share our experiences and ex-  pertise. Our desire to help others maintain competitive advantage in today's ever-changing environment is the driving force behind our success. Our publications include:

- *Logistics and Manufacturing Outsourcing: Harness Your Core Competencies*
- *The Supply Chain Handbook*
- *The Future Capable Company*
- *No Boundaries: Break Through to Supply Chain Excellence*
- *No Boundaries: Moving Beyond Supply Chain Management*
- *Think Outside the Box: The Most Trite, Generic, Hokey, Overused, Clichéd or Unmotivating Motivational Slogans*
- *Goose Chase: Capturing the Energy of Change in Logistics*
- *REVOLUTION: Take Charge Strategies for Business Success*
- *The Genesis Enterprise: Creating Peak-to-Peak Performance*
- *Warehouse Management Handbook — Second Edition*

Audiotape editions are available for some selections. For more information about Tompkins Press or to order books, e-mail resources@tompkinsinc.com. To order books on-line, please visit the publications section of our website at www.tompkinsinc.com.